PRAISE FOR THE IT PAYOFF

"*The IT Payoff* addresses the single most important issue for the future of the information managers and functional managers: The need for a compelling, convincing, disciplined, and well-communicated financial model for IT investments."

—Peter G.W. Keen
author of *The eProcess Edge* and *Freedom Economy*

"This book should be required reading for executives and managers of technology companies—companies like mine that sell new technology to business enterprises. Our customers no longer buy new technology on faith or on unsubstantiated productivity claims."

—Dan Hesse
Chairman, President, and CEO
Terabeam

"Devaraj and Kohli have got it right. They take on one of the most challenging questions that companies are facing in this era of hypercompetition and provide a practical and insightful guide to its resolution. Particularly useful is the attention to issues of measurement, including the tricky intangible outcomes from IT that most firms cannot afford to ignore. I would recommend this book as a must read for anyone interested in leveraging IT investments."

—Varun Grover
William S. Lee Distinguished Professor of Information Systems
Clemson University

"*The IT Payoff* offers staid advice on the investment decision making process. The market may change, your products may change, and your IT investment must be able to roll with the punches. Devaraj and Kohli examine the very issues that keep IT buyers and users up at night."

—Jim Corgel
General Manager, e-business Hosting Services,
IBM Corp.

The IT Payoff

ISBN 0-13-065074-9

90000

9 780130 650740

FINANCIAL TIMES PRENTICE HALL BOOKS

For more information, please go to www.ft-ph.com

Thomas L. Barton, William G. Shenkir, and Paul L. Walker
Making Enterprise Risk Management Pay Off:
How Leading Companies Implement Risk Management

Deirdre Breakenridge
Cyberbranding: Brand Building in the Digital Economy

William C. Byham, Audrey B. Smith, and Matthew J. Paese
Grow Your Own Leaders: How to Identify, Develop, and Retain
Leadership Talent

Jonathan Cagan and Craig M. Vogel
Creating Breakthrough Products: Innovation from Product Planning
to Program Approval

Subir Chowdhury
The Talent Era: Achieving a High Return on Talent

Sherry Cooper
Ride the Wave: Taking Control in a Turbulent Financial Age

James W. Cortada
21st Century Business: Managing and Working
in the New Digital Economy

James W. Cortada
Making the Information Society: Experience, Consequences,
and Possibilities

Aswath Damodaran
The Dark Side of Valuation: Valuing Old Tech, New Tech,
and New Economy Companies

Henry A. Davis and William W. Sihler
Financial Turnarounds: Preserving Enterprise Value

Sarv Devaraj and Rajiv Kohli
The IT Payoff: Measuring the Business Value
of Information Technology Investments

Jaime Ellertson and Charles W. Ogilvie
Frontiers of Financial Services: Turning Customer Interactions
Into Profits

Nicholas D. Evans
Business Agility: Strategies for Gaining Competitive Advantage
through Mobile Business Solutions

FINANCIAL TIMES
Prentice Hall

In an increasingly competitive world, it is quality
of thinking that gives an edge—an idea that opens new
doors, a technique that solves a problem, or an insight
that simply helps make sense of it all.

We work with leading authors in the various arenas
of business and finance to bring cutting-edge thinking
and best learning practice to a global market.

It is our goal to create world-class print publications
and electronic products that give readers
knowledge and understanding which can then be
applied, whether studying or at work.

To find out more about our business
products, you can visit us at www.ft-ph.com

Pearson
Education

The IT Payoff

MEASURING THE BUSINESS VALUE OF INFORMATION TECHNOLOGY INVESTMENTS

SARV DEVARAJ • RAJIV KOHLI

Foreword by Peter G. W. Keen, author of *The eProcess Edge* and *Freedom Economy*

FINANCIAL TIMES
Prentice Hall

An Imprint of PEARSON EDUCATION
New York • London • San Francisco • Toronto • Sydney •
Tokyo • Singapore • Hong Kong • Cape Town • Madrid •
Paris • Milan • Munich • Amsterdam
www.ft-ph.com

Library of Congress Cataloging-in-Publication Data

Devaraj, Sarv, 1966-
  The IT payoff: measuring the business value of information technology investments /
Sarv Devaraj, Rajiv Kohli.
    p. cm. -- (Financial Times Prentice Hall books)
  Includes index.
  ISBN 0-13-065074-9
    1. Information technology--Cost effectiveness. 2. Information
  technology--Management. 3. Capital investments--Evaluation. I. Kohli, Rajiv, 1961- II.
  Title. III. Series.
HD30.2 .D475 2002
658.15--dc21   2002019150

Editorial/Production Supervision: *MetroVoice Publishing Services*
Acquisitions Editor: *Tim Moore*
Buyer: *Bryan Gambrel*
Manufacturing Manager: *Maura Zaldivar*
Cover Design Director: *Jerry Votta*
Cover Design: *Anthony Gemmellaro*
Interior Design: *Gail Cocker-Bogusz*
Project Coordinator: *Anne R. Garcia*

FINANCIAL TIMES

Prentice Hall

Prentice Hall books are widely used by corporations and government agencies for
training, marketing, and resale.

The publisher offers discounts on this book when ordered in bulk quantities.
For more information, contact: Corporate Sales Department, Phone: 800-382-3419;
Fax: 201-236-7141; Email: corpsales@prenhall.com; or write: Prentice Hall PTR,
Corp. Sales Dept., One Lake Street, Upper Saddle River, NJ 07458.

Printed in the United States of America

10   9   8   7   6   5   4   3   2   1

Pearson Education Ltd.
Pearson Education Australia PTY Ltd.
Pearson Education Singapore, Pte. Ltd.
Pearson Education North Asia Ltd.
Pearson Education Canada, Ltd.
Pearson Educación de Mexico, S.A. de C.V.
Pearson Education—Japan
Pearson Education Malaysia, Pte. Ltd.

CONTENTS

FOREWORD

The IT Payoff is all about being a professional. It's a *management* book that addresses the single most important issue for the future of the information services (IS) field and one that will become more and more central to general managers and functional managers: the need for a compelling, convincing, disciplined and well-communicated financial model for IT investments. The IS field has largely lacked all four of the adjectives that precede "financial model" in my previous sentence. Indeed, many executives would argue that it's lacked any sense of financial realism and hasn't had any model.

Historically, to be an IT "professional" meant having training and experience in systems development and project management. Development was the core of any information services organization and technology skills the necessary base for its success. There was very little attention paid to what should have been a priority: *the financial responsibility of true professionals* to ensure effective use of the firm's capital investment in IT. This just wasn't on the agenda. In the close to thirty years that I've taught at major business schools, I can't recall a single course devoted to the topics *The IT Payoff* so lucidly and comprehensively addresses. In the 1980s, the focus of IT education did shift from development to IT-and-competitive-advantage (an almost breathless single word), but the focus was on market share, growth and new product, and service development. Here again, the financial responsibility was ignored. The implicit assumption was that growth would generate return and that competitive advantage ends up on the bottom line.

I recall my own book *Competing in Time*, published in 1986; it did not contain a single page on managing the costs and benefits of the investment. In 1988, I sponsored and published a book, *Getting Business Value from IT*; it sank with little trace. The flood of books about *Net Something* were largely naïve or even irresponsible about the financial side of the dotcom era. Of course, there has for a long time been plenty of discussion of the issues of IT payoff. Much of this has basically been ideological in nature and highly repetitive, centered around the Productivity Paradox, a term coined by an economist skeptic about IT that set the agenda for much of the academic research on IT payoff. (Most economists have been skeptics in this regard.) Little of this work has had any real management relevance. It ignores what I believe is the strength of *The IT Payoff*: attention to the *process* of financial analysis, justification, and communication.

The data the academic work has used has also largely been very dubious; it uses macro level figures that are incomplete and do not reflect the multiplicity of cost elements. IT costs are scattered across many budgets and in my own experience only 20% of them are visible; the rest is what I call the cost iceberg. In addition, the fundamental problem in assessing IT payoff has always been how to attribute value to infrastructures that enable specific applications. At the level of the individual project it's possible to measure return on investment (ROI) in many instances, though even here, it's very difficult to quantify all the "soft" benefits such as "better" service, "improved" communication, and the like. All this is well-known but until the problem of the search for payoff is handled in managerial rather than conceptual terms we will see no more progress in the next ten years than we have in the past ten.

Business executives have long been frustrated by the IT payoff problem. The last 3–5 years have seen several shifts in their view of IT that in my own opinion demand that IS make the financial side of IT its professional core. The earliest shift came from the accelerated move of technology from the periphery of business to its mainstream, first through the massive investments in ERP necessary to end the mass of disintegrated applications and infrastructures that had accumulated over a twenty year period, and second, the emergence of e-commerce as a force that has transformed many industries and is now part of everyday life, regardless of whether or not companies make money from it. Executives now realize that technology is an executive responsibility. In around half the firms I work with, the Chief Marketing Officer or Chief Operations Officer is effectively the CIO. More and more IT investments are led by the business.

The second shift was Y2K. This was a massive and largely unplanned expenditure that in many companies took money away from other priorities. CEOs and CFOs felt they were being forced to write a blank check. Perhaps the business community as a whole might have felt the investment more worthwhile if Y2K had been a disaster instead of a non-event! In any case, when the third shift came, Y2K looked inexpensive. This was the dotcom frenzy. Here, CFOs who had long been concerned about controlling IT costs and ensuring detailed ROI analyses, lost all control. The new blank checks had extra zeros on the end of the figures, with minimal business justification. "Never again!" That's the view from the executive boardroom, a boardroom that knows much more about IT than it did a few years ago.

We are in a fourth major shift: from customized systems development as the norm and packages the exception, to the reverse. The art form of development is now "tweaking" and "chunking"—my own term for how companies now integrate ERP, CRM, legacy systems, and data resources through such tools as C++/Java and XML.

All these shifts subtly, sometimes slowly, inevitably redefine the role of the IS professional. Of course technology skills still matter, but many of these will be obtained from outside, by using integrators and software houses, many will be built in business units, such as data warehousing and CRM expertise. What has changed is the matter of financial responsibility. *Who is responsible for ensuring IT payoff?* If not IS, then who? If, though, IS has the responsibility and leadership, then it had better have the professionalism. The topics of this book are the core of that professionalism. If the business is responsible, it too needs a new management competence. Again, this book provides the grounding for that competence.

The strengths of *The IT Payoff* are its management focus and its inclusion of all the elements of cost, benefit, technology, and business justification. It's marked by its realism and lack of the fogginess of so much of the ideologically-driven work pro or con the Productivity Paradox. It does full justice to the wide research and methodologies that have emerged over the past decades but places them in their business and organizational context. It is simple in the best sense of the term: well-articulated, well-paced, well-reasoned, and not simplistic. It is a very valuable contribution to helping IS people become business professionals and also to aiding non-IT managers in understanding and taking charge of business change, which almost invariably now requires substantial investment in IT as platform, enabler, or support for innovation.

The era of IT as technical development is coming to its close. The era of IT as financial responsibility is long overdue.

—Peter G. W. Keen
Chairman, Keen Innovations,
and Senior Fellow, Differentis
Fairfax Station, Virginia
December, 2001

1

INTRODUCTION TO INFORMATION TECHNOLOGY PAYOFF

"Show me"

—THE UNOFFICIAL STATE MOTTO OF
THE STATE OF MISSOURI, USA

IT PAYOFF: A DIALOG

Bob Graham has been the chief information officer (CIO) of a $2 billion manufacturing conglomerate corporation for 5 years. He is getting ready for a meeting with the CEO, Patricia Donahue, to request approval for a $14 million project leading the corporation's seven strategic business units (SBUs) and the corporate office into the next generation of telecommunications and computer networking. With the profit margins decreasing, Bob proposes to cut computing costs by centralizing financial and planning operations, along with information services, to the corporate office. However, Patricia is concerned with the returns on investment (ROIs). Times are getting tough; revenue is increasing but profitability continues to shrink. Recently she read about companies outsourcing their IT to manage increas-

1

ing costs of IT operations. Intuitively, she *knows* that investment in information technology is strategic and will pay off in
the long run, but she is wondering how she will get the Board to
approve this request given that it approved a $4 million system
upgrade just 2 years ago. At the next board meeting, she is also
taking capital expenditure proposals to upgrade current com-
puter-assisted manufacturing systems for one SBU and a customer relationship management (CRM) system for another.

"Pat, I recognize that we have not done a good job of demonstrating ROI. I also know that there are changes in our business coming down the pike, and I am asking for this funding so
we are prepared for the future," empathizes Bob. Pointing to
the number at the bottom of the top page, Bob makes his case:
"This investment will allow high-speed access to financial
applications for all our SBUs while giving the corporate officers
data to continue company-wide oversight. With the development and maintenance functions at the corporate office, we
can spread the overhead across our member organizations
(MO) and improve quality and reduce costs."

"How long will it take to implement this system?" asked Pat.

"Eighteen to 24 months for the development and implementation," replied Bob.

"And when will the corporation see the impact of spending, given that we will continue to incur costs of our existing
system until the new system is fully operational?"

Looking puzzled, Bob replied "Well, it depends upon how
long it takes the finance department to train the SBUs, and
how quickly the marketing department can utilize this information to negotiate favorable contracts."

"Do you have an ROI on the $4 million infrastructure
upgrade project we did 2 years ago?" asked Pat. "We know that
the speed issue has been resolved and SBUs can run reports
much faster than they used to. The number of complaints is
down. In addition, we are doing a lot more Web applications
through our Intranet," replies Bob, sensing the uphill battle.

While nodding her head in agreement, Pat cannot help but
think about the Board members asking her the question, "How

has this helped business productivity, profitability, or added value to our customers?" At almost the same time Bob was thinking, "I wonder why information resources is being asked to justify the value of the investment. We are the conduits that enable business processes. It is the functional areas that need to develop a strategy, improve processes, and justify that they are working smart."

Does this sound familiar? If you have not been in on this conversation, chances are you will. Each one of us involved in using or deploying IT will probably face the question of this justification issue in one form or other. It is really no different than the questions we ask ourselves when buying a home PC, or that Palm Pilot that we want to invest in after we missed a few appointments. In business organizations, the stakes can be significantly higher and those asking these questions do not buy the argument that it would be nice to have this new information technology. Technology solution providers and consultants also confront IT payoff by their clients who expect to see evidence of benefits from new information systems. An enterprise resource planning (ERP) software vendor or a consulting company has to convince the client that the investment is likely to pay off. Clients will ask for projected benefits to justify the expense.

These scenes are played in the mahogany row and strategy rooms in many organizations. Businesses are looking at IT investments, holding them up to the same scrutiny as other lines of business or acquisitions, looking for ROI. The budgetary belt has been tightening in a capital-constrained business environment. Conflicting findings on IT payoff combined with recent shakedown in e-businesses has further expedited reevaluation of the investment in IT and the resulting payoff.[1] What are the reasons for the senior management to question

---

1. Studies by Strassman (1990) and Roach (1987) have shown that productivity at the economy level has decreased in the last few decades while IT investment has continued to grow. Strassman, P. A. (1990). *The Business Value of Computers: An Executive's Guide*. New Canaan, CT: Information Economics Press. Roach, S. (1987). *America's Technology Dilemma: A Profile of the Information Economy*. Special economic study, Morgan Stanley.

the IT payoff? Is this a recent phenomenon? How can one frame the correct questions to get to the heart of the question? Is it worth investing in information technology? Or does information technology make a difference?

REASONS FOR IT PAYOFF MEASUREMENT

Even when all assumptions of expected IT payoff hold true, the unconvinced manager may ask: How will one know if and when the payoff was realized? Is it measurable? How do we know if there is a payoff at all? Is it due to other factors, such as a strong economy, poor performance of the competitors, or just a better product—and not due to investment in technology?

Corporate managers' concerns when raising questions of IT payoff justification include competing investments and the duration of payoff in addition to the overall state of the economy in which they operate.

COMPETING INVESTMENTS

Just as Pat intuitively felt that IT investment does result in payoff, most executives understand the strategic role that technologies play. It is likely that some have been a player in the implementation of past IT-based initiatives. However, as stewards of the corporations' resources, it is their responsibility to judiciously allocate financial and people resources to all areas of the business. Just as any rational person would, executives want to invest in propositions that show the highest promise of payoff.

All other functions compete with IT to get a piece of the budget pie. Given that the pie is usually a fixed amount, the representatives of each function present its case. Although IT still has the glamour value, it is hard to convince a financial accountant on charm alone. Furthermore, revenue-producing functions in most organizations have a stronger voice than support functions (such as IT). Although many organizations apply usage-based charge-back, strategic IT investment, such as developing an infrastructure, is generally a nonrevenue-producing support function. Senior executives in manufacturing organizations have to decide whether they should invest in more high-precision machines or a CRM system to coordinate supplier–customer relationships. Similarly, a healthcare CEO may have to choose between acquiring the more advanced CAT scan equipment or a cost information system. A transportation company COO may have to balance the available funds to purchase more trucks or a vehicle routing system.

DURATION OF PAYOFF

In considering which investment to choose, senior executives feel pressured by the duration of payoff, that is, how long it will take to see returns on investment. Admittedly, many businesses are focused on the near-term profitability, risk reduction, and tangible business enabling IT. Therefore, information technology investments, such as infrastructure development, that tend to have less apparent and longer payoff duration, may be harder to justify.

OVERALL ECONOMIC PICTURE

Senior managers are concerned that even when there is promise of a payoff, the assumptions may change and the payoff may never be realized. Many companies invested heavily in information technology in the late 1990s and some high-profile failures such as Hershey's and Nike caused some unease in the industry. But the sudden economic downturn in the 2000–01 period, combined by the acts of terrorism in the United States, changed the outlook for the overall economy as well as for demonstrated IT returns on investment. While there are indications that IT budgets have not declined, closer scrutiny of the resulting payoff can be expected. Although firms have little control over changes in the overall economic picture, the payoff justification and planning should take into account such scenarios. The worst thing a firm can do under such market conditions is to stop or roll back investment in information technology, thereby virtually assuring no payoff. During the

1990s' economic recession, progressive organizations utilized the slowdown by diverting resources to reengineer processes, invest in technology, and get ready for economic recovery.

How Has Investment in IT Been Measured Thus Far?

Following is a sampling of approaches for measuring IT payoff. In addition to these, companies can have several homegrown approaches to measuring IT payoff that may be suited to the level of investment or the nature of industry. However, the metrics generally are grouped into three broad categories: profitability, productivity, and consumer value.

Profitability

This approach generally examines financial measures designed to evaluate the "bottom-line" impact of IT investment. Some of the commonly applied techniques are:

Cost–benefit analysis. Cost–benefit analysis entails examining the difference between the costs incurred and the benefits obtained from the investment. Typically, costs are determined as a sum of expenses in the development of the system, including hardware, software, and consulting. Also added are costs such as training, maintenance, customer support, licensing fees, future upgrades, and interfacing with existing systems. Benefits are assessed by the return the system generates back to the organization. However, this gets tricky because the returns are not always tangible. Benefits can be in the profitability, productivity, or consumer value areas. While profitability is easier to measure, productivity gains and particularly consumer value becomes increasingly more difficult to quantify. For a system to be deemed acceptable, the organization expects benefits to exceed costs.

Return on investment. IT professionals like to show ROI because it justifies the information resource function's worth to the organization. Similar to cost–benefit analysis, ROI is measured by the total investment and the benefits obtained, except that the benefits are assumed to be incurred over time. The return, or benefit, is then calculated for a specific time period to generate a percentage on the investment. In this simplified example, if a company invests $100,000 in a system and accrues a benefit of $12,000 per year, the annual ROI would be 12%. This ROI will have to be adjusted for the costs of acquiring the capital and depreciation of the system over time.

PRODUCTIVITY

Productivity measures vary depending upon the nature of the work and the industry. For example, in McDonald's restaurants, the overhead monitor linked with the order-taking register can increase the efficiency of the kitchen staff by 30 seconds per sandwich. Similarly, for a help-desk staff, it could mean three more support calls per hour resulting from a searchable database; and the FedEx delivery person delivers the correct package to the correct address due to a computerized sorting system.

Efficiency. Simply stated, efficiency metrics measure the output of an operation vis-à-vis the resources consumed. If a computer-aided design (CAD) system reduces the time to design an automobile part by a few hours with no additional consumption of resources, it will be considered an efficient system.

Quality. Although quality metrics can be grouped in a class by itself, improved quality of work that reduces rework of the product or service can impact productivity. A manufacturing firm found that even though some of the parts were not strictly up to specifications, most of them would work fine when installed in the assembled product. Through an image of the part, the new information system simulated installation of the part in the final assembly operation of the equipment before recommending the part to be accepted or rejected.

CUSTOMER VALUE

Often the firm investing in the technology does not see direct benefits in profitability or productivity, but instead, the customer benefits from it. So why would an organization want to invest in technologies from which someone else benefits? The reasoning is that if the customer is satisfied, or, better yet, is dependent upon the system, it will lead to greater loyalty and long-term retention. It is easier and cheaper to keep customers you have than to replace them with new ones. In 1999, the University of Notre Dame implemented a high-speed network called *ResNet* to access the campus network throughout its residential halls. One can argue that the tangible benefit that the university accrued was the saving of dial-in phone lines and modems that dormitory students no longer needed to use. However, the expense of *ResNet* was in the millions of dollars. Similarly, FedEx's investment in online package tracking gave the customers online tracking ability. Also, Hyatt hotel customers can track their charges from their hotel rooms. In each case, the investment added customer value more than tangible profitability or productivity for the corporation.

IT PAYOFF: A CASE FOR CONTINUED INVESTMENT?

So why do companies continue to invest in IT when there are issues with obtaining a measurable payoff? There can be many forms of intangible payoffs. Similar to customer satisfaction, organizations have realized that employee convenience leads to satisfaction and loyalty. Many companies now have online benefits administration where employees can enter their vacation or sick hours, and check the balance in their Flexible Reimbursement medical account. Often, organizations invest in new information systems technologies to create a positive market image, even when only a few customers take advantage of it. An example is that of Dr. Jeffery Mader, who has a private dental practice in South Bend, Indiana. The overhead television in each room of his clinic runs self-directed education for various dental conditions. The system also projects real-time images of the inside of the patients' mouth conveyed from a tiny camera on a stick that is inserted. The TV system is linked to the scheduling system and allows the hygienist to make future appointments while the patient is still in the chair. There are few people who take advantage of this feature because, like many of us, they do not have their calendar with them. Yet, the system is impressive and gives the sense to Dr. Mader's patients that he is up to speed on the latest technology.

Even when organizations make productivity gains, they sometimes end up passing some or all of the savings to customers in the form of lower prices or expanded services, or both. Wal-Mart's exemplary inventory management system provided great efficiencies for the corporation, but some of it is passed to the customer in the form of lower prices. One may wonder, why does Wal-Mart invest in an information system and then pass the payoff to the customers, in effect profiting no more than its competitors? This can be explained by Wal-Mart's business strategy to reduce costs, pass on the savings to customers, and increase profitability by increasing sales. Other instances of when continued investment is warranted are the fight for survival in shrinking industries until the "dust settles." U.S. hospitals have seen their profitability drop significantly since the 1990s, yet they continue to invest in information technology. They know that if they can just survive for a few more years while other hospitals close, they will have the systems in place for healthy competition. Several other reasons for IT investment can be difficult, if not impossible, to measure. When improved information systems integrate the new product development process, the investment payoff results in reduced time to market. Similarly, payoffs from knowledge management systems may manifest in the development of new products or the reduction in development costs.

Government or trade regulations also trigger investment in information systems that have little or no potential for improved profitability or productivity to the organization, for example, tracking AIDS-related information or tracking race to satisfy equal employment opportunity commission (EEOC) requirements. Perhaps the most evident example of investment in IT that reciprocated little payoff was the effort invested in testing the information systems for the year 2000 (Y2K) initiatives. Finally, organizations invest in upgrades of software because the vendor may not support older versions.

So, what is the evidence that IT payoff occurs? Why do we keep hearing about the "Productivity Paradox"? Is there such a thing?

2

THE IT PAYOFF PARADOX

*"We see computers everywhere except in the
productivity statistics."*

—ROBERT SOLOW, NOBEL LAUREATE IN ECONOMICS

Webster's dictionary defines a paradox as a statement that is seemingly contradictory or opposed to common sense and yet is perhaps true. *Is IT payoff really a paradox?* Some of the evidence does seem to point to this conclusion. While millions of dollars get siphoned off to IT projects in the hope of improved performance, the payback from these is not in line with expectations. Proponents of the paradox argue that the link between investments in technology and organizational performance has been inconclusive. While some companies seem to provide anecdotal evidence of positive payoffs, several others struggle to obtain the intended benefits. The inconclusive nature of this debate led to the coining of the term "productivity paradox."

Most people have a mixed perception of the contribution of IT. In a keynote address to the International Conference on

Information Systems, Arno Penzias, the former VP and Director of Research at AT&T Bell Labs and a Nobel Laureate, listed a number of studies that had found a negative effect from IT. However, he also stated an example where IT had made a remarkable difference. The New York Metropolitan Transit Authority (MTA) had not found the need to open another airport in more than two decades, even when the traffic had tripled. This, he acknowledged, was due to the productivity gains derived from improved IT systems. IT systems have played a critical role in ticket reservations, passenger check-in, baggage clearance, crew scheduling, and runway and terminal assignments, to name but a few of the applications that enabled the New York MTA to cope with the increasing traffic over the years. Many of us might find ourselves thinking like Arno Penzias did, conceding some cases where IT might be a factor in payoff but still have an overall critical view.

Why is the question of payoff so much more relevant today than ever? It is because the last few years have witnessed an unparalleled growth in investment and applications of new technologies. It is because today 45% of all capital investment in the United States is in information technology. It is because today organizations view investments in technologies as a way to combat competition by simultaneously improving productivity, profitability, and quality of operations. This is evident by the surge in recent years in the number of articles dedicated to examining the payoff from information technologies. Much work was sparked off in this area due to the open debate on the "IT productivity paradox."

FACTORS CONTRIBUTING TO THE IT PRODUCTIVITY PARADOX

ANECDOTAL EVIDENCE

One of the cardinal mistakes in drawing inferences from experience or analysis is the tendency to generalize the findings. In other words, it is our inclination, when we see a particular result, to believe that this applies universally. It is in this vein that we find a lot of prescriptions in the literature on IT payoff. A case in point would be the generalization that ERP implementations can be a nightmare, based on the anecdotal evidence from Hershey's. The candy maker's initial implementation of a $112 million ERP project caused widespread disarray, including shipment delays and incomplete orders. By the same token, the fact that IBM reduced its time to ship a replacement part from 22 days to 3 days is no guarantee that other ERP implementations might yield similar benefits. The bottom line in this argument is that these are all anecdotal experiences likely to be incorrectly interpreted as universally applicable. Yet, when we read contradicting experiences, what remains in our minds is the notion of a paradox.

A SNAPSHOT VIEW

If we were to look at all the studies that were conducted to evaluate whether or not there was a payoff from IT, one common characteristic that many of these studies share is that they examine the payoff question at a certain point in time. In other words, their abstraction of reality is what is captured in a snapshot. Now, this is not such a bad thing if we were looking at the IT application and its payoff after a sufficiently long duration. The truth of the matter is that this is hardly ever the case. Like every other organizational initiative, IT implementations also take time to realize their full potential. Therefore, *when* we decide to examine the payoff becomes very crucial in assessing true benefit from IT. Many studies that have observed a positive payoff from IT have done so after considerable time lags. The reason for the time lag is that the phase immediately after the implementation is one where significant learning and adaptation to the new system occurs. This period will very likely not result in tremendous performance improvements. The objective, in many companies, is to just "hang in there" until the creases are ironed out. The true benefits that will be observed after this initial period might range anywhere from several days to several months, and in some cases even years, depending on the size and complexity of the

IT implementation. Therefore, any evaluation of IT benefits must be cognizant of this time-lagged aspect and assess benefits over time. In fact, our own investigation of the IT payoff phenomena suggests that studies that attempted to track IT payoff over a longer period of time had a higher likelihood of detecting true benefit, if any occurred.

ISOLATING THE EFFECT OF IT

Protech Solutions was a leader in providing IT-based solutions to both service and manufacturing firms. A recent IT implementation was a knowledge management system that helped to capture and reuse the knowledge of the 10,000 workers at Protech. Knowledge management is the concept by which an organization gathers, organizes, and shares its knowledge in terms of resources, documents, and people skills. The implementation did not come easy, nor was it inexpensive. The Knowledge Manager and the CIO of the company were faced with the task of having to justify the new system to the CEO and Managing Director. In the presentation that ensued, they were able to show at an operational level that the percent of new orders for the last quarter, which was the period when the KM system was in place, was 35% higher than the preceding quarter. In more aggregate terms, they also indicated that part of the 85% increase in revenue for the same period last year might be attributed to the new IT system. Do you see the leap of faith in their arguments? The one question that their analyses and similar analyses done in boardrooms over the globe cannot address is "Can you attribute the performance improvement (or decline) to the IT implementation?" This question is the same one that was posed in Chapter 1, when we discussed the reasons corporate managers have on their minds when they raise questions of IT payoff justification. Can we say with a certain degree of confidence that what we observed is due to the IT implementation? In the discussion at Protech, it was clearly not the case. The IT industry was in general experiencing an upswing, and improvements in performance were expected due to this. Management did not buy into the argument that it was the IT system that provided the efficiencies that might have resulted in performance for that quarter being significantly higher than before. The story of Protech is a familiar one. The principal issue encountered is whether we can isolate the effect of IT on firm performance. It does not have an easy answer, because it means disentangling the effect of IT from various other factors such as competition, economic cycle, capacity utilization, and many other context-specific issues. Some of the techniques discussed later in this book address the issue of isolating the effects of IT.

LEVELS OF ANALYSIS

IT payoff studies have been conducted at different levels: economy, industry, and firm, each with different objectives. The economy-level studies attempt to capture the aggregate IT impact for the whole economy, not separating out the high-tech versus the low-tech companies. Industry-level analysis is useful to estimate industry trends in the conversion of IT into business value. The detailed level of the firm offers the advantage of observing the impact of IT while also disentangling it from other factors. In terms of results observed, many IT payoff studies, conducted at the economy level, observed a negative relation-ship between technology-related variables and performance. However, the economic level is also one in which it is difficult to separate the high performers and the low performers. Details about issues such as the companies that faced intense competi-tion, the companies that invested in IT aimed at improving product quality, and a host of other issues are impossible to dis-entangle at the economy level. At the industry level, the results are more mixed, with certain studies documenting a positive impact of technological investments, while other studies detect no significant advantage to IT investments. At the more detailed level of the firm, the results indicate a positive relationship between technology and performance. The trend that emerges from these studies seems to suggest that the more detailed the level of analysis, the better the chance to detect the impact, if any, of a given technology.

AGGREGATED ANALYSIS

One of the reasons that the technology–productivity connection seems elusive is because of an aggregated unit of analysis. That is, technology is implemented at a process level, and we look at the organizational level. This mismatch between the level at which the investment occurs and the level at which we are measuring payoff makes it difficult to isolate the impact of any individual technology.

Thus, recent work in IT payoff has highlighted a new framework to examine the payoff question. The notion articulated is a "process view" of technology investments.[1] Investments in IT lead to assets, which in turn lead to IT impacts; impacts, when aimed appropriately, lead to organizational improvements. The salient feature of the process approach is that investments in IT are likely to show organizational improvements only when the intermediate points—assets and impacts—are directed properly. Just because an organization invests in information systems, this cannot be a guarantee that there will be a measurable effect on the performance. The process view proposes that IT expenditures have to be converted into appropriate IT assets. The appropriate use of IT assets leads to IT impacts, and IT impacts, when positioned competitively, lead to impacts on organizational performance. A more detailed discussion on the process view is presented in Chapter 5.

COMPLEMENTARY FACTORS

Another recent development in IT payoff analyses is the notion of complimentarity. This view suggests that to realize maximum benefit from IT, there needs to be not only an investment in IT, but also an "IT-driven" reengineering of the existing process of achieving a task(s). In terms of complementarity theory, activities are complements if any one of them increases the returns to the others. Based on notions of complementarity,

---

1.   C. Soh and M. Markus, "How IT Creates Business Value: A Process Theory Synthesis," *Proceedings of the Sixteenth International Conference on Information Systems*, (1995, December), 29–41.

Barua and colleagues[2] presented a theory called business value complementarity. One of the arguments put forth, based on this theory, was that investments in IT and reengineering cannot succeed if done in isolation. Since technology and business processes were viewed as complimentary factors, they must be changed in a coordinated manner to improve performance.

DOES THE PARADOX STILL EXIST?

While many believe that the IT paradox is history, since we are able to explain what caused it, there are many others who believe that it is still very relevant. People who belong to the latter camp believe that IT has failed to lift productivity growth throughout the economy. The argument put forth is that productivity growth is more due to an economic cycle than other factors. At times of fast growth, firms work employees harder and, thus, see productivity growth; and in times of economic downturn, the opposite holds true. More important than whether the IT paradox exists today, or is a resolved issue, are the lessons we need to learn from this debate. The factors that contributed to the paradox are factors that we need to keep in mind even today as we evaluate and justify technology investments.

MOVING BEYOND THE PARADOX?

On the positive side of this paradox debate is the realization of the various issues and their interconnection with payoff. Conceptual, methodological, and implementation issues that contribute to the paradox have surfaced. The onus is therefore on the managers and users of technology to be aware of these and not fall into the same trap.

Paradox or otherwise, the last decade has been a witness to IT investments coming under more scrutiny than ever before. In fact, there are many who think that the IT paradox has been

---

2. A. Barua, B. Lee, and A. Whinston, "The Calculus of Reengineering," *Information Systems Research, 7* (1996): 409–428.

resolved. This change in mood is also evident in the words of Nobel Laureate Robert Solow, who initially took a very skeptical view of the contribution of IT, but now has indicated a more positive stance: "My beliefs are shifting on this subject . . . the story always was that it took a long time for people to use information technology and truly become more efficient. The story sounds a lot more convincing today than it did a year or two ago." Another example would be Alan Greenspan, Chairman of the Federal Reserve Board, whose position is evident in his statement, "Information technologies have begun to alter the manner in which we do business and create value, often in ways not foreseeable even five years ago."

If the paradox has been resolved and the connection between IT and payoff been established, then are managers investing more in IT? Not really, claim Kenneth Kraemer and Jason Dedrick, from the Center for Research on Information Technology and Organizations (CRITO).[3] In fact, they believe that this *is* the new paradox! If indeed IT investments provide rich dividends, if in fact IT investments provide higher returns than non-IT investments, then the current investment level in IT is much lower than what is needed. They argue that this could be the next paradox that challenges both economists as well as policymakers. We may be past the first IT paradox—a case can be made for why a connection between IT investment and performance was not observed. Our knowledge has vastly increased in this process and we can now drill down to some of the most critical factors that might cause a break in this linkage. Issues that have come to the forefront are that objectives need to be set up front and time-based criteria for measuring results need to be established. However, there might still be cases where a payoff was not observed due to the mismanagement of the IT investment. One of the key ingredients to ensure that this does not happen is to have a solid foundation that starts with a sound technology strategy.

---

3. J. Dedrick and K. Kraemer, "The Productivity Paradox: Is it Resolved? Is There a New One? What Does It All Mean for Managers?," University of California Irvine, Center for Research on Information Technology and Organizations (CRITO), (2001), Working Paper ITR-168.

3

THE STRATEGIC ROLE OF TECHNOLOGIES

Information technology is often thought of as a solution to problems facing business. The attitude of some business managers is that if we throw enough computing power at them, we can resolve most business problems. Although that may appear to have been the case in some situations, it most likely involved a strategic evaluation and alignment of IT with business strategy before the payoff occurred.

WHY IS STRATEGY IN IT PLANNING IMPORTANT?

IT is a tool, and when used in the context of a sound business strategy, can yield significant payoff. Contrary to general belief, the technology does not have to be very sophisticated for a payoff. Peter G.W. Keen, a prominent thinker in IT management, points out that when all companies essentially have access to the same information technology resource, the difference in competitive and economic benefits that firms gain from information technology rests on a management difference and not on a technology difference.[1] The technology is generally available to other competitors as well, yet some organizations reap far greater payoffs. Similar to the strategy of the arrangement of pieces on a chessboard, the management difference constitutes placing pieces of technology in the pursuit of a strategic objective.

Consider the example of gas stations that offered customers the ability to pay by a charge card at the pump. There was no new technology involved in this service; it was merely extending the card-charging service that was available inside the glass doors to the gas pump. The result: customers were happier because they did not have to go inside and stand in line. The gas stations' cost was low because they did not have to hire more gas attendants to accept payment. Yet, in those early days, gas stations with this facility were charging a few pennies more per gallon. That's the payoff of reconfiguring an existing technology.

In another example, Pizza Hut, a popular chain of restaurants, linked their telephone caller identification (ID) facility to a personal computer-based database. As the call came in, the number from their caller ID retrieved the customer's name and address, including driving directions, purchase history, and even preferences. The result: customers referred to by name were impressed, the time to take the order was significantly reduced because address and directions did not need to be asked, and additional sales were generated when the person taking the order prompted for additional items. Examining this investment in IT, Keen's words ring true. The caller ID as well as the PC-based database technology used by the pizza restaurant is widely available to any individual or business. It was the man-

---

1.   Peter G.W. Keen, *www.peterkeen.com*

agement difference, that is, the manner in which Pizza Hut arranged the pieces to create a system, that led to the payoff.

In both cases, the exploitation of IT was based upon a sound strategy—providing customers with the service they want and improving efficiency by reducing costs. In spite of phenomenal successes of IT by some organizations, others have squandered the opportunity to gain strategic advantage by failing to develop a sound strategy or mismatching the strategy with the needs of the customer.

Greyhound, the leading U.S. passenger bus transport company, revamped its reservation system. However, after spending a significant amount of time and budget, the system was a failure. First, the reservations program had a number of screens with a built-in credit card approval process, resulting in a longer wait for the passengers. Furthermore, the strategy to serve the customers using IT failed to recognize that many passengers who travel by bus do not make advance reservations and do not possess credit cards.[2]

WHAT IS STRATEGY?

Michael Porter, a Harvard professor and one of the most influential business strategy theorists, argues that businesses need to get back to using IT as part of corporate strategy as opposed to an inward-looking operational role. He also places the responsibility on the IT professionals to know the customer, to understand the manufacturing process, and to take a business view of the company.[3]

Technology management is similar to managing financial investments. Just as the investment strategy is guided by personal goals, IT investment should be managed by the strategic goals of the company. When a new opportunity arises or the

2. R. Tomsho, "How Greyhound Lines Re-engineered Itself Right into a Deep Hole," *Wall Street Journal,* 20 October 1994, 1.

3. "Competing Interests," *CIO* magazine, Interview: Michael E. Porter, 1 October 1995, 63–68.

investor's goal changes, so does the investment strategy to take advantage of such opportunities. Similarly, the business strategy should be realigned when a new technology is recognized or when a new business opportunity arises.[4] If strategy is so important, how should businesses go about strategizing?

DEVELOPING A STRATEGY

Many leading researchers and consultants have developed approaches to implement strategy within organizations. There is no one universal approach guaranteed to result in a successful strategy. You may find it helpful to examine the steps in the strategy development process and then select those that suit your business and market position.

As a first step, a business should assess the state of the competition and its position in the marketplace. We refer to this step as looking outward. A realistic understanding of the market layout combined with looking inward and assessing its own strengths and weaknesses will allow the organization to recognize a successful strategy. Then, the management can decide how it wants to stake its place in the market. Due diligence for each set of options in the strategy should be studied by examining the risks and opportunities associated. Many an investment has been abandoned because more attention was placed on the risks and not enough on future opportunities.

LOOKING OUTWARD

A strategy is as much an exploitation of the competition's weaknesses as it is an exploitation of your strengths. It is that fine blending that creates new opportunities. Align with

---

4. T. Erickson, et al. "Managing Technology as a Business Strategy," *Sloan Management Review,* Spring 1990, 73–83.

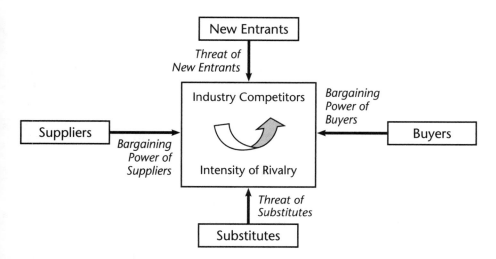

FIGURE 3.1 Porter's five market forces.

enabling technologies and a supportive organizational infrastructure, and you have a lethal product.

Among the most widely applied approaches for market analysis is Michael Porter's five forces (Figure 3.1).[5] The state of the competition, according to Porter, depends upon (1) the threat of substitute products; (2) the threat of new competitors; (3) the intensity of rivalry among competitors; (4) the bargaining power of suppliers; and (5) the bargaining power of customers. Although Porter's work was not written specifically for information technology strategy, it speaks as well to IT strategy as to other disciplines. As you consider these five forces, think how IT strategy can affect the forces in your industry. In the following paragraphs we prompt you to evaluate opportunities for your IT investment strategy. Using Porter's framework, we raise questions that link IT investments with corporate strategy so that payoff can be maximized.

The threat of substitute products can change the competitive nature of the industry. Can IT lead to new products or ser-

---

5. Michael E. Porter, *Competitive Strategy: Techniques for Analyzing Industries and Competitors.* (New York: Free Press, 1980).

vices? Can your company be a threat to the market? Examine what new technologies can render the current product(s) obsolete. Similarly, the threat of new competitors entering the market can change the rules of the market. New competitors usually come with new ideas, revised paradigms, and, like the revolutionaries, are dissatisfied with the way the industry operates. Due to dissatisfaction with the pricing of IT services, lack of IT's link with business strategy, and opportunity to stay technologically current has led many IT professionals to break off and compete with their former mentors and employers. Former IBM professionals who recognized that customers wanted enterprise-wide solutions started the company SAP, which specializes in providing enterprise resource management. Most vendors at the time, including IBM, were not providing integrating solutions in which the functions of the entire enterprise could be integrated. Application Service Provider (ASP) outsourcing companies are gaining market recognition because the pricing of software has not kept up with the needs of the customers. Recently, the popularity of Napster, the Web music download service, highlighted the customer's need for picking and choosing individual recordings, rather than having to purchase the complete album. Unless the music industry responds to this customer need, new business will continue to cater to this demand, to the detriment of the established music business. On the other hand, a new entrant catering to the needs of the market can gain a significant share of the market.

The intensity of rivalry among competitors is an indication of the rough road ahead for a business looking to make it in a new industry. The pneumatic tube industry is not quite as glamorous as some new economy technology industries. Yet, the level of competition among the three major players can be described as intense.[6] To succeed in intensely competitive industries, the new entrant should have a novel idea or approach to gaining customers, or a remedy for the weaknesses of the industry.

---

6. Pneumatic Tubes, National Public Radio, Morning Edition, April 23, 2001.

The buying power of customers and suppliers can affect the nature of competition if you happen to be a supplier or a customer, respectively. When is the customer or the buyer in a position to bargain? General Motors was in a position to negotiate with its suppliers to join its Electronic Data Interchange (EDI) system. Those suppliers that were not able to go through the transition were to be phased out. Why was GM able to bargain? In this case it was GM's size and the volume of business it gave to its suppliers. Similarly, smaller hospitals joined to form a consortium and bargain for competitive prices from large medical equipment suppliers. Suppliers with leverage over their customers can benefit from investment in IT and thus bargain to keep favorable conditions. The ROI from IT investment under these conditions will be enhanced if the firm chooses to link it with its market position.

LOOKING INWARD

Having examined the competitive position of the industry, the company should assess its own strengths and weaknesses, opportunities and threats, also called SWOT analysis. The purpose of looking inward is to match the internal strengths with opportunities of the industry and create something of value. Only then will the investment in IT be expected to pay off. Payoff results from a value-added product or service. Such service includes both types of customers: internal and external.

Often the opportunity for IT payoff lies within. In the early days of long-distance telephone deregulation, customers were thrilled to have MCI as an alternative to AT&T as a long-distance service provider. However, many were dissatisfied with the billing and customer service part of the operation. This is a prime case for internal IT investment in billing systems and training customer-service representatives.

Porter's value chain analysis (VCA) provides a framework to examine each area of the business that can be targeted for

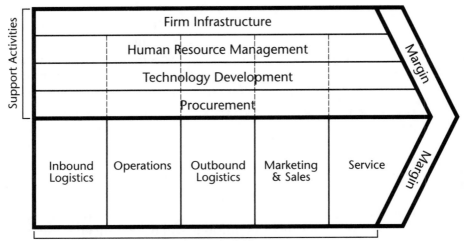

FIGURE 3.2 The generic value chain.

IT investment (Figure 3.2).[7] VCA lays out primary and support activities that a business performs in the course of producing a product or service. As in the case of Porter's five forces previously discussed, you may view each of these activities in the context of IT capabilities assessment.

Inbound logistics, the first primary activity, evaluates the process of inbound activities such as raw material to convert to finished products, inventory for processing, or deposits in the case of a financial institution. In many cases, the inbound activity involves human intellectual activity such as a computer program or remote monitoring and diagnostics, or data processing as in credit card operations. Nevertheless, the organization should consider its current sophistication and future strategic opportunities. For instance, can sharing the inventory information with suppliers help reduce stockouts? Will a telecommunication network link to software development firms in India allow the organization to gain access to a large pool of IT professionals?

7.   Michael E. Porter, *Competitive Advantage: Creating and Sustaining Superior Performance.* (New York: Free Press, 1985).

Operations activity involves receiving the inbound raw materials and executing the process of converting them into finished products. Operations may appear to be less glamorous than the other primary activities, but it offers an opportunity to be innovative and add significant value for the customer. An innovative process in steel manufacturing, use of high density metal alloy in auto parts, and providing feedback to engineering and design professionals can lead to significant cost savings as well as a high-quality product.

Similar to the inbound, the outbound logistics involves efficiently dispatching finished products and services out of operations to the customers. Often, an investment in one channel can lead to payoff in both inbound and outbound logistics. Automated Teller Machines (ATM), designed to facilitate outbound logistics (dispensing cash), also facilitate inbound activity (deposits). Similarly, an online travel reservation system can help a customer locate an appropriate flight (inbound logistics) and in the end deliver an electronic ticket (outbound logistics).

Marketing and sales can offer significant opportunities for IT investment payoff. Targeted advertising and market research, developing sales leads, and managing customer relationships are some examples of IT-based initiatives.[8] A contract modeling system for Trinity Health's hospitals helps determine the profitability of their contracts with insurance companies. Trinity Health managers use historical data along with the modeling system to assess the expected costs of a potential contract before they bid.[9] McDonald's analyzes the sales data gathered each day through a Decision Support System (DSS) to learn what product lines are selling better than others. Its marketing managers then assess the effectiveness of advertising campaigns and plan for new marketing efforts.

---

8. R. Kohli and J.N.D. Gupta, "Strategic Application of Organizational Data through Customer Relational Databases," *Journal of Systems Management*, 44 (1993): 22–41.

9. S. Devaraj and R. Kohli, "Information Technology Payoff in the Healthcare Industry: A Longitudinal Study," *Journal of Management Information Systems*, 16 (2000): 39–64.

Standing by the product and providing after-sales service has always been valued by customers. However, the escalating cost of personalized service has kept many businesses from delivering at expected service levels. However, this is where an organization has a great potential for winning and keeping customers. While there is no substitute for personalized service, IT investment in customer relationship management (CRM) systems can help identify the problem, match the skills of the person providing the service, and schedule the service. Otis Elevators, through their remote monitoring of elevators, can test, diagnose, and even fix a problem. In addition, the company can schedule a technician to arrive at the location at the same time a spare part arrives by overnight delivery.

A company's activities are frequently just as important as its primary business activities for delivering value to the customer. In the support role these activities facilitate the operation of primary activities. The corporate IT infrastructure involves the free flow of data to carry on business activities. A corporate-wide email and appointment scheduling system is supported by a sound IT infrastructure. KPMG's Shadow Partner provides access to corporate "knowledge" from a client's site so that a consultant can take advantage of the resources available throughout the organization. Similarly, AT&T reduced office space costs by providing "virtual offices" to its employees who spent much of their time traveling. A virtual office consists of an electronic infrastructure with capabilities for voice mail, email, and fax, allowing access to corporate databases from anywhere in the world. Without an effective IT infrastructure, such widespread access is difficult to achieve.

Similarly, human resources management (HRM) facilities support the activities of recruiting and retaining good people. Training, certification, and recognition help keep employees motivated to serve the organization well. Technology development is an activity that can have long lags in payoff. However, it is crucial for organizations to stay current with new technologies and to introduce them into business operations after they have been tested. Finally, the procurement, as a secondary activity, is like housework. You don't see it until it is not done. When procurement fails to get the needed parts or materials, everything can come to a standstill. In highly competitive markets, the procurement services group is a strategic partner at the planning table. When the profit margins are thin, an effective procurement function can contract for favorable pricing and stable delivery of goods and services.

Having assessed the SWOT of the organization and identified areas of strategic opportunity, we need to understand how we are going to measure the payoff. This includes understanding where to look for the impact of strategic investment, identify the IT, and conduct due diligence.

WHAT TO LOOK FOR

Recent research[10] has shown that the impact of IT investment is not always evident in the profitability of the firm. This may have contributed to the controversy over the productivity paradox. Instead, the payoff can be reflected in other ways such as higher efficiency or increased customer value. For various reasons, these gains may not appear in the bottom line of the firm. How can a company be more productive and not increase profitability? How can a company not see gains in its profitability when it has satisfied customers?

Lorin Hitt of the Wharton School at the University of Pennsylvania and Erik Brynjolfsson of the Massachusetts Institute of Technology found that IT has increased productivity and created substantial value for consumers. However, they did not find evidence that these benefits have resulted in significantly higher profitability. In other words, Hitt and Brynjolfsson find that there is no inherent contradiction between increased productivity, increased consumer value, and unchanged business profitability, because in competitive industries businesses may pass on the savings from improved productivity to their cus-

---

10. L. M. Hitt, and E. Brynjolfsson, "Productivity, Business Profitability, and Consumer Surplus: Three Different Measures of Information Technology Value," *MIS Quarterly, 20* (1996): 121–142.

tomers. An understanding of how and whom technology is likely to affect will lead to useful metrics of IT payoff.

CONNECTING THE DOTS

With the understanding of the market and the opportunities within, organizations develop a strategy to exploit market opportunities. The strategy takes into account the enabling technologies. Finally, prior to placing the strategy into action, organizations should conduct due diligence. We will discuss enabling technologies and techniques used to conduct due diligence in greater detail in later chapters.

4

FAILURE
ANALYSES

*"Failure is only the opportunity to begin again
more intelligently."*

—HENRY FORD

Our earlier discussion on the IT paradox presented the case advanced by some analysts and commentators that IT investments do not return their value to a company in the form of a measurable payoff. The mere fact that there was no measurable payoff does not imply an IT failure because the objective of IT investment might be to protect market share or avoid legal exposure.

On an anecdotal level, the examples of IT failures are plenty. Oftentimes, failures are very valuable teachers—teaching in a manner deeper and more lasting than if the project was a breeze-through success. This chapter is about looking at lessons of IT project failures in other organizations and learning from them.

TIMING IS EVERYTHING

The timing of the IT implementation decision is one of the critical factors that affects the success or failure of a project. Sometimes, just pushing back the implementation by a week might have had very different consequences. Case in point: Whirlpool Corporation's implementation of an SAP ERP system. According to SAP AG officials,[1] Whirlpool should have delayed the "go-live" date by a week knowing that certain red flags had been raised. The red flags involved two batch-processing transactions that were taking a long time to feed into the decision support database and the customer service system. However, Whirlpool wanted to take advantage of the holiday weekend and kick off the implementation before the end of the year, and went ahead with the implementation. The rest, as they say, is history. The result was a shipping system that went completely awry and had shipments sitting in warehouses with some stores having to wait six to eight weeks before receiving their shipment. The lesson learned is that it is much more important to have a complete product than to be on schedule, especially in light of red flags observed. This is pertinent advice because we see many projects go live with red flags.

UNREALISTIC EXPECTATIONS

Another factor relates to top management's belief about the extent to which the system and people can perform to carry through a project of mammoth proportions. This is especially true in times when every move seems to be a good move, for example, in the "dotcom era." *CIO* magazine[2] presented a detailed report of a company called Close Call (a pseudonym to protect the identity of the company) that fell victim due to

1. Stacey Collett. *ComputerWorld*, 8 November 1999.
2. Lauren Gibbons Paul. "Anatomy of a Failure," *CIO* magazine, 15 November 1997.

the CEO's unrealistic expectations. Close Call was in the business of telemarketing and catalog sales. The CEO wanted to implement a data warehouse that would fully integrate the various call centers. The lure of integrated data flow and data on demand was too much to resist. However, the CEO believed that getting the data warehouse up and running in 3–4 months was just a matter of "getting the right people for the job." The Information Systems (IS) department was already stretched and, therefore, outside help was sought. The expectations, with regard to resources as well as time required, were very unrealistic. After the pilot project turned out to be a debacle, the entire data warehousing project was canceled. While the initial budget slated was for $250,000, the team spent nearly $750,000. Half of Close Call's IS staff quit their jobs after the project. The company's stock price lost more than two-thirds of its value during the period. The reason for the failure, as stated by a consultant for Close Call, was because they attempted too many technology projects at the same time, a case of biting off more than they could chew. The lesson, in this case, is to set realistic expectations of IT implementations. A cross-functional team might provide a more balanced outlook and serve to temper expectations.

MANAGEMENT SUPPORT

Top management's support is critical for projects to be successful. However, in large organizations spread across the globe, it is easy to lose sight of this factor. *CIO*[3] reports the case of a company that lost 50% of its market capitalization due to top management's failure to implement a global information technology strategy. The failure cost the company approximately $500 million dollars at a time when most established companies were demonstrating strong gains on Wall Street. The company was a market leader in the industrial services business, with

---

3. James M. Spitze. "Inside a Global Systems Failure," *CIO* magazine, 1 February 2001.

offices in almost all developed countries. There were several IT issues that were the cause for a lot of agony and that also affected the bottom line. First, customer queries on order status took several days to respond compared to only a few minutes the competition needed to accomplish the same task. Second, orders from a single customer with locations in different countries were processed by separate systems. This created unnecessary redundancies and made it difficult to provide an integrated statement to the customer. Finally, pricing was extremely complex. Often, a service that was customized was far less profitable than expected.

A globally accessible, up-to-date information system was planned that would replace the legacy systems that were the cause of the company's problems. Despite the development of a detailed plan to address these problems, there was no buy-in from executives in the various divisions across the globe. The lesson learned is one that we emphasize later in the book as well: top management support and buy-in can often be the critical difference between successful IT implementations and the others.

EXPLICIT PAYOFF METRICS

Many IT implementations are decided on the intuition of top management. While intuition and "gut feeling" are managers' best friends, they have to be backed by objective analyses and metrics if the project is to be a success. In the example of the telemarketing and catalog sales company called Close Call (discussed previously), another crucial mistake was the lack of clear objectives during prelaunch of the data warehousing system. Explicitly outlined objectives serve two vital functions. First, they help in the development of feasibility studies to ascertain the realistic costs and benefits from the implementation. As discussed above, many times the cause for IT failure is unrealistic expectations. This step will lend some objectivity to this process and thereby temper overly optimistic (or even pessimistic) viewpoints. Second, the establishment of prelaunch metrics will help identify the contingencies involved, as well as aid in getting the "buy-in" from different groups. Another good practice might be to do an iterative rollout. That is, specify that partial functionality will be provided by a certain date, followed by additional functionality at a later date, and so on.

INFRASTRUCTURE

Technology strategy failures can be either management failures or technology failures. Mail Boxes Etc. (MBE) exemplifies the case of grand strategy but the failure of technology.[4] MBE launched an Internet-based shipping system called iShip that was the brainchild of MBE President and CEO Jim H. Amos, Jr. The aim was to position MBE as the preferred shipping partner for e-tailers. The infrastructure comprised building a satellite network to connect the 3,500 domestic franchises with corporate systems, an Internet-based point-of-sale system and the iShip manifest system. The system would only require the phone number of returning customers and would be able to recall all the customer information, including recipient information. This, it was hoped, would make the customer feel very special and make life easier for the customer by not requiring address information during repeat visits. While it was a well-intended technology strategy, the infrastructure did not work as planned. Connections to the remote computer system were very difficult to establish and, even when successful, were very slow. Part of the problem was that the satellite hookup was slow even compared to cable modem technology. Indeed, many MBE franchisers went back to a decade-old DOS-based system to enter orders rather than the Internet-based iShip system.

Another illustrative example is that of Furniture.com,[5] whose executives promised shoppers 24-hour browsing as well as a six- to eight-week delivery time on everything from table

---

4. Darwin, May 2001.
5. Stephanie Overby, "Survivor III," *CIO* magazine, 1 May 2001.

lamps to 10-piece bedroom ensembles. The first part of the plan went very well—that of attracting more customers. The site attracted about 1 million users a month. However, while executives of Furniture.com built its brand name at an astonishing pace, they neglected to create the infrastructure to support it. Customer complaints filed with the Better Business Bureau in Worcester, Massachusetts, jumped from 1 in 1999 to 149 in 2000. Most complaints were delivery problems, followed by product quality and bill disputes. Why did this happen? The company did not create an appropriate infrastructure that would factor in the logistics and costs of shipping such a bulky commodity across the country. Besides, they did not have a platform that would track the orders. The company closed its doors on November 6, 2000, and filed for bankruptcy. The company was done in by promises to customers that its infrastructure could not allow it to keep, such as the six- to eight-week shipping time, free delivery, free returns, and so on. According to David Pyke, Professor at Dartmouth's Amos Tuck School of Business Administration,[6] while free shipping and returns, low prices, and lots of variety could make customers happy if the promises were fulfilled, the company could not make money like that.

ARE YOU READY FOR INTEGRATION?

"If you're not careful, the dream of information integration can turn into a nightmare."

—THOMAS H. DAVENPORT[7]

The promise of many recent technology implementations is that of a unified front, a single data warehouse, information integration—all phrases to suggest that life will be a lot simpler through integration. In fact, at the heart of every enterprise

---

6.   Stephanie Overby, "Survivor III," *CIO* magazine, 1 May 2001.

7.   Thomas H. Davenport, "Putting the Enterprise into the Enterprise System," *Harvard Business Review*, 1 July 1998.

resource planning system is the notion of integrating the various functions within an organization.

If integration comes with all the touted benefits, then where is the danger in integration? Integration comes at a cost. By costs, we don't just mean financial costs. In ERP implementations, these might be the costs of not having a certain kind of customization that we were used to. These might be the costs of having the business be dictated by the logic of an overarching integrated ERP system. These might be the costs of certain local systems not being able to talk to the centrally integrated system.

Industry analysts claim Hershey's experience with ERP is a classic example of the problems associated with integration of various packages.[8] Hershey implemented a wide-ranging array of SAP AGs ERP modules simultaneously with companion packages. These included a planning and scheduling package developed by Manugistics as well as a pricing promotions package developed by Siebel Systems. The challenge was to integrate the three disparate systems seamlessly. That's no easy task, by any measure. The integrated system was implemented in July 1999, when retailers began ordering for back-to-school and Halloween sales. While Hershey's plants continued to churn out Kisses and candy bars, the inventories were piling up in the warehouses instead of on store shelves. Product inventories were up by 29% compared to previous year's levels due to order processing problems arising from the implementation of the new system. By mid-September the company said that the new system was causing delays in shipments and deliveries of incomplete orders. By November, Hershey announced a 19% drop in third-quarter profits when CEO Kenneth Wolfe said that system fixes were taking longer than expected and requiring more extensive changes. Eventually, after a series of fixes to the ERP system as well as a revamped distribution facility, Hershey made sure that the problem did not recur the next year.

---

8.   Craig Stedman. *Computerworld*, 1 November 1999.

TRAINING

Training is often treated as a stepchild of an information system implementation process. "It is surprising that companies spend millions of dollars on hardware and software, but assume that the system will work by itself," says Dave Piotrowski, an executive with an e-business company. They assume that if the system is implemented well, the users will learn how to use it. On the contrary, many systems that fail within a few weeks of implementation do so because few people know how to use it. Organizations should identify users, schedule trainers, determine location, and conduct training as part of the project plan. Training should utilize actual data and business scenarios and coincide with users' ability to put training into practice immediately upon returning to their jobs. Organizations should utilize consulting resources for training and knowledge transfer. Often, outside consultants depart after a "successful" implementation and leave the system to the users who are not equipped to carry out daily business activities using the new system, let alone troubleshoot any problems that might arise.

In this chapter, we have outlined what we believe are "critical" contributors for many IT implementation failures and juxtaposed them with examples of businesses that we have observed in the last 2 years that were exposed to these factors. At this point, it may also be useful to rethink the implicit assumptions of the productivity paradox debate. What about those cases in which there is no financial payoff from IT? Are we right in labeling these as failures? The IT investment objectives of a firm can be defensive, such as to protect market share or to avoid legal exposure. For example, the recent reductions in revenue in the healthcare industry have brought significant new investment in IT. Given the competitive marketplace and shrinking reimbursement for services, many healthcare organizations will consider IT payoff as positive if their losses are curtailed. We see a similar challenge to reach a financial break-even point in the U.S. steel industry due to falling prices in the world market and not necessarily due to any failure of technology. Similarly, technology investment as protection from a potential loss can also lead to an ostensible lack of IT payoff. A recent example of IT investment for legal protection is the Year 2000 (Y2K) project. The Y2K investment added very little to the firms' competitiveness but protected them from potential legal exposure. There is also evidence that IT may not always lead to improved profitability, rather, it may manifest itself in improved efficiency or consumer value.[9]

Therefore, many situations on the surface might appear to lack payoff, however, by delving deeper we may realize that the payoff was in another area, or maybe just the fact that the business survived while much of the competition fell on the wayside. Also, on many occasions, there might not have been a benefit to the organization but benefits may have been passed on to the customer. These are all cases where really there was a payoff from IT.

---

9. Hitt, L., and E. Brynjolfsson, "Productivity, Business Profitability, and Consumer Surplus: Three Different Measures of Information Technology Value," *MIS Quarterly, 20* (1995): 121–142.

5

A PROCESS
PERSPECTIVE

Mismeasurement of the IT payoff is often seen as one of the culprits for spawning the productivity paradox. Experts believe that many payoff studies have used inappropriate measures or applied blunt tools to measure the impact of IT. Our own analysis indicates that there is great diversity of measurement tools applied in past IT payoff studies.[1]

The issue of (mis)measurement breaks down into two primary camps. First, those who believe that the payoff from IT investment should be measured by the change in the outcome, such as higher sales, greater market share, or reduced costs. This is called the variance approach. In the second approach,

1.   R. Kohli and S. Devaraj, "Measuring Information Technology Payoff: A Meta-Analysis of Structural Variables in Firm Level Empirical Research," Working Paper, University of Notre Dame, 2000.

called the process approach, IT investment is measured through the process of IT's use in creating the outcomes. While both camps are interested in measuring payoff, the process approach says that the payoff should be measured by intermediate steps such as creating proper IT assets and their impact on business processes before their impact on the organization. We'll discuss the variety of tools in a later chapter; however, here we discuss these two basic payoff measurement approaches, each proposed by a theory.

LET'S TALK THEORY

Variance theory proposes that in measuring IT payoff we should look for conditions that are "necessary" and "sufficient." Necessary conditions are those that are required for the payoff to happen. Sufficient conditions are those that explain most IT variances in payoff. Once we identify these conditions, we look for the difference in payoff as those conditions change. For instance, when a corporation makes an IT investment in the implementation of an EDI system and the necessary employee training, the payoff outcome is measured in dollars of net profit, while EDI implementation and training are the two conditions assumed to affect net profit.

The variance theory proposes that we examine the change, or variance, between net profit before the investment with the EDI implementation and training after the investment, after controlling other factors such as unit sales, seasonal adjustments, and general economic conditions, which can also influence net profit. Most past studies in the literature have applied the variance theory and statistically examined such variance. In the above example, the variance theory approach considers both technology investment and training as necessary and sufficient conditions for causing a change in net profit.

On the other hand, the process theory proposes that we examine how the investment is made and the sequence of events that lead to the change in net profit. It works on the assumption that while we know the "necessary" conditions (such as EDI implementation and training) required to achieve an IT payoff, we need to ascertain if those conditions are "sufficient." Net profit may also be affected by changes made by partnering organizations to ensure that accurate data are captured. In other words, the process of IT investment may consist of several factors, including some that are unknown or not easily quantifiable, and can facilitate or hinder the eventual payoff.

ADVANTAGES OF VARIANCE AND PROCESS APPROACHES

The advantage of the variance approach is that it is based in statistically rigorous methods to assess the impact. It also provides the quantitative models for forecasting the impact of IT investment and the resulting payoff. Quantitative models of the variance theory also advance theory by establishing a mathematical relationship between variables as well as the size of the effect—that is, it examines how net profit varies when the investment level increases by 10%. The variance approach is well suited for a large sample size (e.g., greater than 50 data points) of survey-based or economic analyses where IT investment effects at the industry- or economy-level need to be assessed.

On the other hand, if the focus of the payoff examination is one company or a small number of organizations, the process approach is better suited to provide a detailed case-based analysis. Such analysis enables studying the context of the IT investment, the expectation for its success, and other, less obvious factors that might influence the outcome. For instance, we know that internal political alliances have a bearing on what projects get priority within organizations, and therefore the necessary resources for implementation. Although not formally communicated, political pressures often influence the outcome of IT-based initiatives, something that is more likely to be discovered in the examination of IT assets created and IT impacts in the process-based case study. Unless this was a predefined variable, variance-based approaches are likely to miss this "sufficient" condition of IT payoff.

Another advantage of the process approach is seen in cases when there is little or no payoff observed. A variance approach might indicate that there was no payoff from the investment but provides no further clues, whereas a process approach might possibly identify at what point in the process there was a misfit or misdirection. As was illustrated in Chapter 4 (Failure Analysis), learning about the causes of failures will improve the chances of success for future initiatives.

Process approaches are also useful for understanding the causality linkage in IT spending. For example, the reason for the organization's increased IT spending can be to protect a losing market share, or the past mismanagement of IT resulting in the loss of market share. Given that variance-based analysis does not differentiate between the order of events, the process approach can establish a sequence of events to determine an appropriate action.

PROCESS APPROACH: A DISCUSSION

Soh and Markus summarize the differences between the two approaches and build upon past frameworks that implicitly propose using the process approach in measuring IT payoff.[2] Based upon the findings, they suggest that IT expenditures combined with proper management create IT assets, the appropriate use of which leads to IT impacts (Figure 5.1). It is only after such IT impacts are realized that one should expect payoff to the organization. Consider the creation of assets and the subsequent use of IT assets as stewarding the IT benefits to the next step in the organizational value process. The impact of IT investment on organizational performance, however, is contingent upon the competitive dynamics of the industry and the organization's

2.   C. Soh and M. Markus, "How IT Creates Business Value: A Process Theory Synthesis," *Proceedings of the Sixteenth International Conference on Information Systems*, (1995): 29–41.

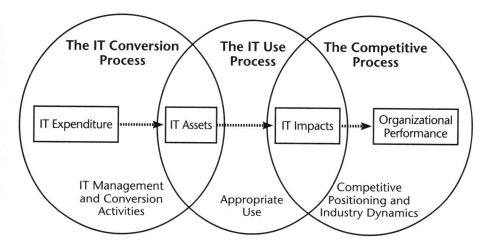

FIGURE 5.1 Process approach to IT organizational impact. *Source:* Soh and Markus (1995).

position in the marketplace. For instance, due to the competitive nature of the industry, gains resulting from improved processes and technology in the personal computer industry are generally passed on to the end-customer through lower prices.

As illustrated in the next section, the process approach opens up the "black-box" of IT investment–payoff linkage and enables us to understand the importance of complementary investments made to ensure successful IT investment.

It is not our intention to imply that the variance approach cannot examine each of the steps listed in the discussion above. Given a valid and consistent set of metrics, the variance approach can be quite effective. However, until we get to a point where we know what these complementary investments are, and how best to measure them, the process approach offers an effective means to examine the IT payoff issue. Soh and Markus's assets–impacts framework also serves as a checklist to ensure that the steps are understood and dealt with in seeing the IT investment through to its conclusion. Now that we understand the benefits of the variance and process approaches to IT payoff, let us examine a scenario where the process approach was applied.

PROCESS APPROACH: AN APPLICATION

Business process reengineering (BPR) was the wave of the 1990s when most companies invested significant amounts of resources in redesigning the processes and the way they do business. These processes ranged from customer relationship management to order fulfillment, from designing aircraft parts to dissemination of information within the organization. Examples of BPR's spectacular success in improving processes include enormous improvements in the accounts payable process at Ford Motor Company[3] and CIGNA Corporation's success in improving customer service and quality while reducing operating expenses.[4]

However, there have been as many cases of BPR not fulfilling initial expectations. So, the question remains, Does BPR benefit the organization? In studying this question, Kohli and Hoadley, at the Lattanze Center for Information Studies in Baltimore, began a study in 1995 to understand how organizations measured BPR outcomes.[5] They surveyed about 200 companies that had conducted BPR. However, the survey approach fell short of accomplishing the goal. The reasons: First, companies defined BPR in different ways ranging from incremental improvement to radical change in the process, therefore, an apples-to-apples comparison could not be made. Second, the expectations from BPR results varied significantly within organizations, therefore, what was success in one organization could be considered a failure in another. Third, the metrics for measurement varied vastly among processes and organizations, ranging from measuring customer satisfaction to return on investment (ROI) to reduction in cycle time. It

3. Michael Hammer and James Champy, *Reengineering the Corporation: A Manifesto for Business Revolution*. (New York: Harper Business, 1993).

4. J.R. Caron, S.L. Jarvenpaa, and D.B. Stoddard, "Business Reengineering At Cigna-Corporation—Experiences and Lessons Learned From the 1st 5 Years," *MIS Quarterly, 18* (1994): 233–250.

5. R. Kohli and E. Hoadley, "Towards Developing a Framework for Measuring Organizational Impact of IT- Enabled BPR: Case Studies of Three Firms." Working Paper University of Notre Dame, 2000.

was clear that when there are no clear definitions of the target metrics, the variance approach would fall short.

This is where the process approach came in. Three organizations were then selected to study the "process" of measuring BPR. The results from the process approach indicated that firms that focused on one of the objectives—improving productivity, increasing profitability, or providing customer value—were more likely to see BPR benefits to the organization. Another finding was that when firms treated BPR as a black box, the results were often based on faith rather than fact. Therefore, firms that methodically examined the process of BPR experienced expected gains. Third, process owners tried to maximize the local payoff from BPR, without regard for the overall impact on the firm. Due in part by the reward and recognition systems, in some cases the improvement in one process came at the detriment of another process. The process approach revealed instances in which assets for creating significant BPR were created, and did indeed add value at the process level, yet the impact on the organization was negligible. For instance, a state-of-the-art order entry system ensured that the orders were taken accurately and efficiently and then forwarded to the order-fulfillment division. While the order-entry system demonstrated significant improvements in the speed of order taking, the organization did not benefit much because those orders would simply wait in the queue for fulfillment. Now it took the order fulfillment function more time to sort the queued orders and increased the number of errors.

COMBINING PROCESS AND VARIANCE APPROACHES

There is no reason why the process and variance approaches cannot be combined to blend the strengths of the two approaches. In fact, some experts have proposed and done just that. In a remarkably well-executed study, Tridas Mukhopadhyay and his colleagues at Carnegie-Mellon University examined the payoff from implementing EDI at the Chrysler

Corporation.[6] The study estimated the dollar benefits of improved information exchanges between Chrysler and its suppliers, resulting from the use of EDI. Applying the process approach, they examined how Chrysler shared information with its suppliers to achieve reduced inventory levels. As with the above BPR example, Mukhopadhyay and his colleagues were concerned whether inventory reduction was achieved at the cost of higher transportation costs between Chrysler and its suppliers. Following the identification of this issue using the process approach, they collected and analyzed premium freight in addition to regular transportation and inventory costs through the variance approach, thereby accounting for the true improvement.

Anitesh Barua and his colleagues at the University of Texas at Austin refer to a similar approach at the two-stage model through which intermediate variables at the application level can be studied, prior to the impact at the firm level.[7] They also suggest that the process approach in measuring IT payoff becomes more meaningful when combined with the complementary intermediate variables.[8] BPR is also one of the complementary initiatives facilitating IT payoff. In our own research we have found support for this argument. We found that although proper IT investment is likely to pay off, its impact is enhanced when the investment is complemented with carefully planned BPR.[9] We found that BPR played a role in not just amplification of IT's impact on profitability but also on the quality of the services.

---

6. T. Mukhopadhyay, S. Kekre, and S. Kalathur, "Business Value of Information Technology—A Study of Electronic Data Interchange," *MIS Quarterly, 19* (1995): 137–156.

7. A. Barua, C.H. Kriebel, and T. Mukhopadhyay, "Information Technologies and Business Value—An Analytic and Empirical-Investigation," *Information Systems Research, 6* (1995): 3–23.

8. A. Barua, C.H.S. Lee, and A. B. Whinston, "The calculus of Reengineering," *Information Systems Research*, 7 (1996): 409–428.

9. S. Devaraj and R. Kohli, "Information Technology Payoff in the Healthcare Industry: A Longitudinal Study," *Journal of Management Information Systems, 16* (2000): 41–67.

Barua argues that much of the literature has focused upon doing the BPR "right," as opposed to doing the "right" BPR. The "right" BPR includes investing in and tracking the right intermediate variables such as customer lead times and satisfaction, and percentage of rework, which in turn will improve the bottom-line.

So what is the benefit of learning about the process and variance theories in the IT payoff context? When would one approach be more appropriate? The benefit of understanding these approaches is to decide how to measure the payoff so that true benefits can be measured. You may be measuring metrics that are not impacted by the IT investment, or measuring too soon and before the impacts have manifested. Conversely, measuring processes that show impact but do not benefit the organization can be a waste of time.

If the IT investment is a one-time investment, such as that in the Year 2000 (Y2K) testing, the variance approach can be best in assessing the payoff. Either the investment in IT paid off or it did not. However, if the investment is ongoing or is to improve past IT investment, it may be useful to know what conditions facilitate or hinder the payoff. These conditions could be cross-functional training, greater integration with other information systems, or easy-to-use computer interfaces.

Summary

In summary, the path to IT investment has to be clearly understood before it can be determined what data are collected and analyzed. You should not hesitate to scrutinize the details of the IT investment process by asking the following questions:

1. What factors lead to the IT investment?
2. What assumptions were used prior to the investment?
3. What was the working relationship among the responsible people?
4. Were measures of success outlined?
5. What assets were created?

6. What complementary changes in training, rewards, reporting, and so on, were made?
7. What intermediate variables were affected?
8. How were the intermediate variables linked to the organizational impact?
9. Was there an impact at the intermediate level?
10. Were there competitive factors that affected the impact at the organizational level?

Through the process approach, we can expect to find if the investment was proper, if the assets were used appropriately, and if the organization experienced an improvement. If this were to be the case, was the improvement in productivity, profitability, or customer value? However, the process approach will not resolve all payoff issues and neither will it improve the IT payoff on its own. The payoff depends upon the complimentarity of activities and assets. These complementary activities and assets include providing people with appropriate skills, training, reward mechanisms, physical infrastructure, suitable technology, software, timely and useful communications, setting up proper procedures and policies, a well thought-out strategy, and directed application of these efforts.

It is clear that the traditional return-based financial measures are just one of the criteria by which IT payoff can be measured. The process approach unearths the rest of the criteria through which true payoff can be measured in a balanced manner by accounting for other outcomes, albeit many eventually affect the financial bottom line. Along these lines, Kaplan and Norton at Harvard University have developed a balanced scorecard (BSC) approach to measuring organizational performance. The next chapter discusses the BSC approach.

6 TECHNOLOGY PAYOFF METRICS— BALANCED MULTIPLE OBJECTIVES

"When you can measure what you are speaking about, and express it in numbers, you know something about it, but when you cannot measure it, your knowledge is of a meager and unsatisfactory kind."

—LORD KELVIN

What is a metric? *Metric* is a term that relates to measurement. The objectives of establishing metrics are for tracking and evaluating performance, benchmarking, feedback, and organizational improvement. Measures can be ROI on a new decision support system or the number of lines of error-free code for an IT solutions provider. Very simply, it is a characteristic of a system, organization, or process that can be measured and expressed in numbers. The two broad categories of IT metrics are *financial metrics* and *operational metrics*.

Financial metrics are driven by costs and have traditionally been the focus of the accounting and financial functions in any organization. Operational metrics, on the other hand, capture performance related to the core functions of the organization. For example, for a healthcare organization the financial metrics might be patient revenue, net income, gross income, and so on, while operational metrics for a cardiac ICU might be number of procedures, length-of-stay of patients, mortality, customer satisfaction, and so on. In a manufacturing context, the financials are typically cost numbers for various categories, while the operational metrics might be number of production runs (flexibility), rejection and rework rate (quality), and parts per hour (efficiency). These measures are the focus of the functional managers and supervisors. In reality, managers monitor both financial and operational metrics to feel the pulse of the organization.

We often find a managerial preoccupation with tangible measures such as cash flows, ROI, and so on, and that these measures play a dominant role in the selection or retention of technologies. Many a discussion on justification of technology is centered around these tangibles. Just because the intangibles are more difficult to get around, it does not downplay their role. Many times, an application service delivers no real profit, but serves other, less tangible values such as keeping up with similar services offered by competitors, providing customer relations value, and so on. Also, in many instances, the only advantage of a new technology might be the flexibility to manufacture a broader range of products down the road. So, does this mean that we should not invest in this technology since it provides no obvious improvement in ROI over an existing technology? Certainly not. The type of environment and competition should be examined, and if the likelihood of product innovation is very real in the next few years, then it makes absolute sense to make the investment in the technology that provides the flexibility to expand the product line, even if the potential is not fully exploited today. Other intangible measures include quality, responsiveness, and innovation. While quality provides a benefit that might be difficult to quantify at first, we will outline techniques in later chapters of the book that will allow you to assess the impact of improved quality on financial performance of a company. Flexibility, on the other hand, is an option that a company may or may not want to exercise in the future. But, the knowledge that we have the ability to exercise this option is in itself a benefit from a technology that provides additional flexibility. Similarly, the ability to respond quickly to changing customer demands or needs can help retain future business.

IMMEDIATE VERSUS LAGGED METRICS

One of the major reasons we are unable to detect payoff from IT is because we are looking at metrics at the wrong point in time. In other words, we are looking at immediate metrics. Consider the following example. A system of hospitals implements a new decision support system (DSS) that enables it to negotiate contracts more effectively. An assessment is undertaken of the benefits of the system. Investment in the DSS is weighed against the benefits in terms of the contracted amount for a given month for all the hospitals. Finding no positive correlation, and in fact, a negative correlation, was a source of utmost concern for management. The IT department was having a difficult time justifying the investment in the DSS for no apparent benefit. The crux of the issue in this real-life situation is that immediate metrics were examined. A more detailed study of the situation suggested that negotiated contracts take about 2–3 months to show up on the financial statements. Since all the numbers for the justification analyses came from the financial statements, an examination of immediate metrics is certainly not going to show any benefits. In fact, further analysis conducted using time-lagged metrics revealed the actual benefit of using the DSS for contract negotiation.[1] The analysis showed that there was indeed a positive correlation and that benefits from investing in IT were derived after a 3-month time lag.

1. S. Devaraj and R. Kohli, "Information Technology Payoff in the Health-care Industry: A Longitudinal Study," *Journal of Management Information Systems, 16* (2000): 41–67.

PRODUCTIVITY, PROFITABILITY, AND CUSTOMER VALUE

In their award-winning study, Hitt and Brynjolffson[2] presented evidence that the payoff from IT need not always reveal itself in metrics that are related to productivity or profitability of the firm implementing the IT. Most all work prior to that had an extensive focus on measures that represented various forms of productivity or profitability. They demonstrated that many times benefits accrued by companies from IT implementations are passed on to the customers. Therefore, it was equally important to assess the value of the IT investment to customers. The metrics that represent this third category have been largely ignored because they are external to the company. However, we should be careful to also acknowledge that every organization has multiple stakeholders, and that benefits from IT may be reaped by stakeholders outside the organization.

While productivity, profitability, and customer value would be the first places to look for IT payoff, there are instances when payoff metrics go beyond these three dimensions. For example, IT implementation to counter the Y2K problem is an example where traditional metrics might not have yielded positive payoff, however, significant IT investments were called for to shield against the possibility of a potential breakdown of the IT machinery. Another example of moving beyond traditional metrics is the case of introduction of new technologies. Initial investments and efforts are geared toward protecting market share more than any kind of efficiency or profitability dimensions. Furthermore, due to competition for gaining customers, IT investments can lead to greater market share but reduced profits. Therefore, the traditional performance measures may actually show a decline in profitability because of the additional expenses incurred to acquire new customers.

---

2. L. Hitt and E. Brynjolfsson, "Productivity, Business Profitability, and Consumer Surplus: Three Different Measures of Information Technology Value," *MIS Quarterly, 20* (1995): 121–142.

Regardless of the spectrum of metrics chosen for examination, there needs to be a balance between them—a balance that can be achieved through the balanced scorecard approach.[3]

A BALANCED AND INCLUSIVE APPROACH

We advocate a balanced approach to determine the range of metrics to be tracked and monitored. While financial measures worked well during the industrial era to measure performance and gauge the leadership position of a company, this measure alone is not sufficient in today's environment. To stay competitive, businesses today have to rely on a number of measures, including financial and operational measures. One of the ways of achieving this is the balanced scorecard. The balanced scorecard is a set of critical factors that, when measured and managed properly, give companies a distinct competitive edge. It includes financial measures such as ROI and earnings per share (EPS) that tell the results of past actions. It ties the financial measures with operational measures for customer satisfaction, internal processes, and innovation and learning activities of the organization. By studying and managing operational measures, an organization can get a good notion of future financial performance. In that sense, an understanding of the balanced scorecard enables us to appreciate the relationships between financial and operational metrics.

The balanced scorecard helps managers view performance in several areas simultaneously. It makes managers focus on a small set of critical measures that most likely drive performance. The scorecard forces senior managers to consider all the important operational measures together and let them see if improvement in one area is achieved at the expense of another. The balanced scorecard allows senior managers to view their business from four important perspectives.[4]

---

3. Robert S. Kaplan and David P. Norton. "Putting the Balanced Scorecard to Work," *Harvard Business Review*, (September-October 1993).
4. Ibid.

- How do we look to the customers? (customer perspective)
- At what must we excel? (internal perspective)
- How do we continue to improve and create value? (innovation and learning perspective)
- How do we look to the shareholders? (financial perspective)

By narrowing the number of measures used, the balanced scorecard avoids information overload while at the same time giving managers a short list of current and future performance. Numerous companies, such as Apple Computer and Advanced Micro Devices, have benefited from the use of balanced scorecards. Figure 6.1 shows an example of a balanced scorecard.

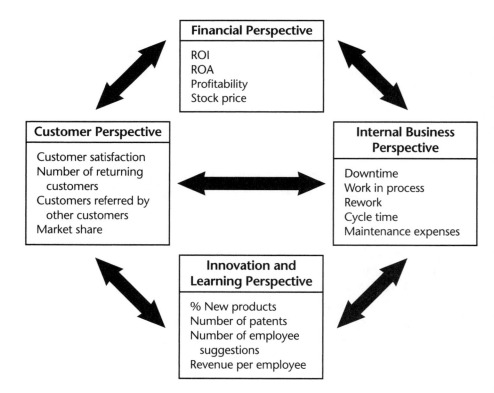

FIGURE 6.1 An example of a balanced scorecard.

CUSTOMER PERSPECTIVE

Maintaining good relationships with customers is critical to a business's survival. Even one customer with an unpleasant perspective or experience of the company can cost the company several hundred customers. With the current ease in which information is transferred and through word of mouth, a company's reputation can be hurt if it does not view itself through the eyes of the customers.

Customers' interests are generally assessed along four dimensions: time, quality, performance and service, and cost. The *time* between which the customer places an order to when the company actually ships the product has to be closely tracked by the company. *Quality* measures the product's defect level as perceived by the customer. *Performance* and *service* measures relate to how the company's products or services help in creating value to the customers. *Costs* are indicative of the internal efficiency of translating inputs into outputs or services.

Customer satisfaction assumes even greater consequences in the context of new technology implementations. The literature on technology acceptance states that two perceptions of users that are of critical importance in satisfaction with any technology are: (1) What is the perceived ease-of-use of the technology? and (2) What is the perceived usefulness of the technology? The answer to both these questions can be assessed from customers and holds the key to user acceptance of technologies. Studies of online shopping have found strong evidence supporting this line of reasoning.

INTERNAL BUSINESS PERSPECTIVE

It is important for companies to know the areas or critical factors in which they have to excel to stay on top of the competition and to satisfy customer needs. The second dimension of the balanced scorecard gives managers an opportunity to focus on those internal operations that enable them to satisfy customer needs. The measures that reflect these internal operations are derived from the processes that have the greatest impact on customer satisfaction, such as factors that affect delivery time, quality, and productivity.

The irony, with regard to this category of measures, is that, while in most companies it is very likely that a host of operational metrics are tracked, very little is actually achieved by way of these metrics in offering directions for improvement. We noticed that in one manufacturing plant, in excess of 80 metrics were tracked, but were buried in reports that nobody read. Unless operational metrics are *used* to assess past and present directions, strategies, and goals for the future, companies cannot benefit from using a balanced scorecard approach.

INNOVATION AND LEARNING PERSPECTIVE

The above two categories of measures of the balanced scorecard constitute areas that companies consider most important for competitive success. However, due to the changing landscape of business, a company that was highly successful during one period may find that it has lost heavily to competition during the next. This is the reason why it is very important for companies to make continuous improvements to their existing products and processes while at the same time introducing new products and services with expanded capabilities. Innovation measures on the balanced scorecard address the company's ability to develop and introduce new products rapidly. These new products might indeed constitute a significant part of future sales. Companies have to continuously improve and cannot rest on past achievements. Companies can focus on two or three areas that have to be constantly improved and set out measures to monitor these areas.

Innovation is the lifeblood of technology companies. Today, a company cannot rest on the laurels of past success. Change is a rule of business. Therefore, a technology such as a flexible manufacturing system that allows workers to work on innovations and changes easily must be recognized and factored in the payoff equation.

Many managers believe that companies go through cycles of growth. They reach a plateau and have to determine what they have learned and what should be their next targets going forward. This sanity check needs to be done by companies, especially at times when growth bubbles burst and companies confront bearish conditions. It is a time to take stock, evaluate the past, and plan for the future. Network Appliance is a good example of a company that built its market from the ground up with an entirely new concept: a storage appliance. Now, at the pinnacle of their achievement, with a new market defined and the appliance concept moved from a radical idea to a mainstream approach to storage, the challenge to their product managers is taking the technology to the next level.

FINANCIAL PERSPECTIVE

Since financial performance is a key factor in determining a company's worth in the eyes of shareholders and other outsiders, senior managers have to be ever-mindful of the bottom line. Even if the above three scorecard measures indicate good performance, the ability of the company to translate operational performance to improved financial performance is critical. The drafters of the balanced scorecard need to lay out what would become of the excess capacity, improved cycle time, and other such improvements that might come about as a result of better operational performance. They should define measures that would capture any redundancies or wastage that would thereby lead to better financial performance. Companies should strive to show how improvements in quality, delivery, and innovation will translate into higher market share or better operating margins. For the balanced scorecard to be a success, companies should learn to make such explicit linkages between operations and finance.

FINAL THOUGHTS ON THE BALANCED SCORECARD

The balanced scorecard enables a company to regulate its management processes and focuses the organization on implementing a long-term strategy. It provides senior managers with a central framework around which they could revise, if need be, each piece of the company's management systems. In the past, performance metrics have served primarily as control mechanisms, the scorecard emphasizing strategy and vision, not control. Due to constantly changing business conditions, the scorecard sets goals, but does not set out guidelines or behaviors needed to achieve those goals. By providing a dashboard of metrics that include financial, customer, internal process and innovation, and organizational learning perspectives, the balanced scorecard helps managers understand interrelationships between these perspectives. This broader outlook helps managers view the organization as a whole and what works best for it rather than an overemphasis on any particular perspective.

While the balanced scorecard was originally designed for the organization as a whole, many of its benefits can be reaped by examining the IT payoff question as well. For example, looking at the broad spectrum of metrics—internal and external, financial and operational—and their interrelationships before and after an ERP implementation, would be a very worthwhile exercise.

RECOMMENDATIONS

Following our review of the balanced approach to metrics, we conclude this chapter with a few recommendations based on our experience with measuring IT payoff within organizations. First, we recommend that to the extent possible, data for IT payoff analysis incorporate contextual metrics. Such context includes the business strategy preceding the investment; implementation factors such as firm culture, skill mix, incentive structure, and conflict resolution; or degree of product and process integration with IT and the extent of business process reengineering (BPR). The context of IT investment can also provide insights into the competitive environment, leading to a method for measuring IT payoff. Such contextual information can also assist in determining the granularity of the data needed for analysis, such as monthly, quarterly, or annually. For instance, in a highly competitive environment of electronic commerce or online trading, IT investment will almost always require shorter time frames for capturing and analyzing payoff than in traditional businesses. The commonly used annual data for analysis is likely to miss key changes in the organizational impact resulting from IT investment.

Second, we recommend that researchers attempt to gather longitudinal data that extends well beyond the initial implementation. IT projects can have extended development cycles followed by training and implementation, which may obscure the overall impact of the investment in IT if longitudinal data are not gathered. Furthermore, an opportunity to examine and isolate the points of impact during the process of implementation is amiss in cross-sectional data. The advantages of cross-sectional data are that it is easier and cheaper to collect, and the analysis is relatively simple. It may be well-suited for studies that examine the impact of a specific technology or an organizational initiative with a known beginning and ending. However, for studies that examine the overall impact of IT investment on the firm, a longitudinal approach provides comprehensive data to examine appropriate effects. Longitudinal data also provide the opportunity to uncover interesting trend or cyclical phenomena.

Third, we extend Hitt and Brynjolfsson's[5] view that the impact of IT needs to be independently measured by examining productivity, profitability, customer value, and the entire balanced scorecard. They contend that although related, the three outcomes should be examined separately. In an examination of 370 large firms, they found that IT may be increasing productivity and consumer surplus, but this increase is not necessarily leading to above-normal business profits. In a competitive marketplace, the retention of a customer base and protection of market share is a pragmatic reason for IT investment, yet such

---

5.   L. Hitt and E. Brynjolfsson, "Productivity, Business Profitability, and Consumer Surplus: Three Different Measures of Information Technology Value," *MIS Quarterly, 20* (1995): 121–142.

gains are less likely to show a significant immediate impact on financial statements. Similarly, an improvement in efficiency can help offset increasing raw material costs or decreasing sale prices, such as reimbursement for healthcare services, yet are not likely to show a significant direct impact on the profitability of the organization.

Finally, we recommend the process view proposed by Soh and Markus[6] to identify appropriate IT assets and impacts prior to examining organizational payoff. We propose an additional step, *targeted analysis,* during or before IT investment. Targeted analysis refers to a deliberate effort on the part of the organization to identify, prioritize, and target areas of IT investment.[7] We suggest that, prior to IT investment, firms should undertake a concerted effort to examine whether investment in IT will improve the chances of creating appropriate IT assets. Businesses are known to fail even as some of their business processes improve because they invested in the wrong processes. An economic value added (EVA) analysis, which will be described in later chapters, for the IT investment will help determine the importance of the IT-enabled process to the firm and the ability of the investment to return more than its cost.[8] We suggest that IT assets should be targeted toward a specific process or objective before an investment is made. We recognize that firms conduct cost–benefit analyses prior to IT investment; however, such analyses are generally limited to efficiency goals and not to the strategic and competitive advantage that IT investment is capable of producing.

Organizations will find that certain metrics are unique to their industry and make more sense than those commonly

---

6. C. Soh and M. Markus, "How IT Creates Business Value: A Process Theory Synthesis," *Proceedings of the Sixteenth International Conference on Information Systems*, (1995): 29–41.

7. M.L. Markus and C. Tanis, "The Enterprise Systems Experience—From Adoption to Success," In R. W. Zmud (Ed.), *Framing the Domains of IT Research: Glimpsing the Future Through the Past.* (Cincinnati, OH: Pinnaflex Educational Resources, 1999).

8. Peter G.W. Keen, *The Process Edge: Creating Value Where It Counts,* (Boston: Harvard Business School Press, 1997).

used. A balanced metric approach that is accepted by all involved is more likely to paint a broader picture of IT payoff and give a sense of the overall return on the IT investment to the senior management.

INTERVIEW WITH GUENTHER MOECKESCH, CEO, SKYVA INTERNATIONAL

How should a customer of SKYVA's flexible value chain software approach IT payoff?

Guenther Moeckesch (GM): They should look for payoff in three areas—cost for development, cost for the implementation, and cost for the long-term benefits you can achieve from deploying a value chain solution.

How does a customer compare the savings of flexible value chain software to standard ERP solutions?

GM: The best way to realize savings is to let the customer build his or her own process—with a flexible template that dramatically reduces the number of steps for developing the process solution. The cost to the customer is significantly less than other software because the customer deploys the final product using standardized components. In other words, this approach reduces the costs because we have automated the creation of the software process itself, and that makes us so unbelievably fast. We find that this model-based foundation and componentized software is favored by our customers.

Is the cost higher at the implementation level because the customers have to spend time in customizing and deploying it?

GM: This is a very interesting question, but the answer is exactly the opposite. Generally an ERP business process reengineering takes about 20 percent of the budget and then the customer spends 80 percent of the budget on implementation and working with consulting firms to examine the processes and confirm that the solution will work. In my experience you have to do the business process redesign moderately by relying upon components and reducing implementation costs. When it comes to the implementation with a flexible value chain solution our experience shows that, depending upon the complexity, one can achieve a cost reduction of 50 or 60 percent.

One year after implementing a flexible value chain solution, how does, for instance, an automobile manufacturer assess the value of IT investment?

GM: That was the third step, the benefits. There are some traditional measurement schemes. One is cost reduction resulting from a manufacturing process that works. The second is inventory reduction resulting from running a dynamic manufacturing process. The third set of benefits occurs after you have combined your profit, generating manufacturing with your supply chain and transfer processes. Organizations can benefit by running down or reducing the overall order to the delivery costs.

Typically, organizations have one ERP solution each for the order processing, manufacturing, outsourcing, and transportation of goods. In addition to the cost of implementing each application, there are costs of adapting the business processes to the specific solution. With a flexible value chain solution, such as SKYVA International's, organizations implement a complete business process—call it supply chain or call it demand chain or value chain—it is basically one end-to-end solution regardless of the underlying system. And that's the biggest advantage we have seen with our customers' IT investment payoff—because it's a business process that doesn't end at the end of manufacturing or at the end or the beginning of transportation and is reflected in efficiency and productivity of their business processes.

Guenther Moeckesch, CEO of SKYVA International, founded the company in 1996 with a vision to improve the way software was built and delivered to customers—a vision of an IT world where "the business process is the application." Dr. Moeckesch brought to market his idea to provide software for creating value chain applications based on a company's unique processes, improving a company's ability to plan, execute, integrate, and evaluate its business across all components of its value chain. Prior to founding SKYVA, he was Head of Development for Process Industries and Logistics SAP, a major ERP software firm. He received his doctorate in business engineering at Karlsruhe Institute of Technology.

7 THE TECHNOLOGY CURVE

"Knowing when to get off the old curve and jump onto the new is the secret of staying ahead of the competition."

—RICHARD FOSTER

Sergei Bubka, a famous Russian pole-vaulter, broke the world pole-vault record, clearing 6 meters in the Paris International Track and Field Meet in 1985. He was asked if he ever expected to clear the 7-meter mark. His response was, "No, there will have to be another technical revolution before that height can be reached."[1] His response implied that there's only so high that one can jump using a bending fiberglass pole. This is a classic example of the limits of technology. Every technology has a limit up to which point it can be harnessed and significant competitive advantage derived from it. But after the limit is reached the companies that realize this and

---

1. Richard Foster, "When to Make Your Move to the Latest Innovation," *Across the Board,* October 1986.

make a switch to the next technology are the ones that will have a sustained competitive advantage.

A tool that can be used to assess the maturity of a technology is the technology S-curve, which is also referred to as the technology curve. It charts the benefits that might accrue from technologies as a function of the maturity of the technology. In many technological environments, paybacks from technology depend on the position along the technology curve. In the initial stages, there is a lot of experimentation and less payback. In the steep portion of the curve is the highest payback, which is a period of high technology improvement. Following this is the flat part, technology maturity, where any extra investment is not likely to provide further benefits. The business that succeeds is the one that jumps the curve to the next generation of the technology at this point.

The essence of the technology curve is the argument that there are limits to technologies, and it is vital to recognize when a technology has reached its limit. When this happens, it becomes very difficult for additional effort and investment to translate into higher payoff. While a few businesses are good at recognizing this limit and making the jump, most continue to cling to old technologies. But that is not a surprise, because it might even be counterintuitive to let go of an existing technology that is successful. So the key to staying competitive, from a technology curve standpoint, is for companies and individuals to realize when the technology plateau has been reached and make a transition to the next technology.

Companies such as Smith-Kline realized the concept of "limits" to reap significant benefits. Sir James Black rejected conventional drug screening approaches, resulting in the discovery of Tagamet for the treatment of ulcers.[2] The development of Tagamet put Smith-Kline in a leadership position in the industry.[3] It was an understanding of the "tyranny of numbers" and the limits on the number of connecting wires that

---

2.   Richard Foster, "When to Make Your Move to the Latest Innovation," *Across the Board,* October 1986.

3.   Ibid.

led Noyce and Kilby to develop a completely new process and product that eventually became the semiconductor chip.[4] Conceptually, how does the technology curve provide value to technology evaluations over other methods such as standard ROI calculations? Many technology evaluation models that are used for justifying technologies are, in a sense, static. They view technologies as interventions that have a certain cost associated with them and certain benefits accruing from them that are constant over the life of the technology. The technology curve brings to this picture the dynamic nature of technology—that benefits might actually depend on the point at which you are observing the technology. Thus, at a very fundamental level, the value in utilizing the tool of technology curves is to incorporate the reality of the dynamic nature of technology adoptions and implementations.

IS THERE EVIDENCE FOR THE EXISTENCE OF TECHNOLOGY CURVES?

Technology curves have been observed across a variety of industries. Semiconductor manufacturing, jet engines, fertilizers, and communications are a few examples of cases in which this phenomenon has been documented. For instance, the reliability of various integrated circuit (IC) technologies has been studied. As the components became more integrated, the system reliability increased significantly, making the newer technologies a source of competitive advantage. For this example, the family of S-curves for the various forms of technologies might look like those presented in Figure 7.1. As a concept, even if the S-curve exists, it serves little purpose if we are not able to chart the course of a technology that is of interest to us. Therefore, we present some detail on the steps to be followed in drawing an S-curve. Charting the technology curve will allow you to assess the degree of payoff that can be expected based on the stage of technology maturity.

4. T.R. Reid, *The Chip.* (New York: Simon and Schuster, 1984).

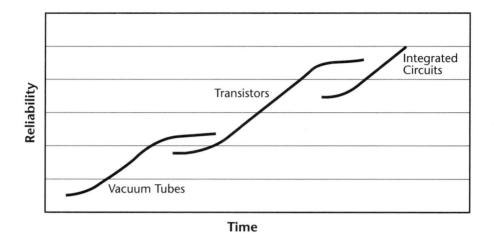

FIGURE 7.1 Technology S-curves.

DRAWING AN S-CURVE (ADAPTED FROM FOSTER[5])

Step 1. Identify the relevant axes. On the vertical axis (Y axis) is the performance criteria that is of interest to and valued by the user of the product. On the horizontal axis (X-axis) is a measure of effort (research and development). For example, in the telecommunications industry the performance criterion might be the speed of transmission achieved measured in bauds. The X-axis might constitute historical data on the R&D effort that went into achieving certain levels of performance.

Step 2. The second step is to identify the limit on technical performance. Oftentimes, a useful intermediate step is to understand the limiting mechanism that will then shed light on the limit on performance. For example, in the case of a chemical catalyst, the limiting mechanism might be the surface area available for reaction.

---

5. Richard Foster, "When to Make Your Move to the Latest Innovation," *Across the Board,* October 1986.

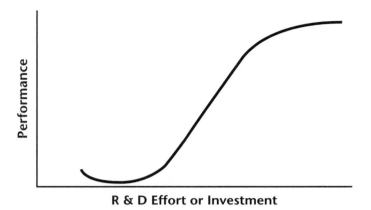

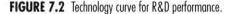

R & D Effort or Investment

FIGURE 7.2 Technology curve for R&D performance.

Step 3. Historical data on performance criteria as well as the extent of technical effort is plotted on the axes. While the more accurate the technology S-curve will be with a greater number of data points used, three to four points, coupled with information about the limit, can be sufficient to draw a relevant S-curve. An example is shown in Figure 7.2.

IMPLICATIONS

Our discussion of the technology curve and some of the literature[6,7] in this area leads to the following implications for managers and users of technology.

PAYOFF DEPENDS ON THE POSITION ON THE TECHNOLOGY CURVE

One of the most significant implications of the technology curve is the realization that the extent and nature of payoff

6. Richard Foster, "When to Make Your Move to the Latest Innovation," *Across the Board,* October 1986.
7. T.R. Reid, *The Chip.* (New York: Simon and Schuster, 1984).

from technologies depends on their position on the curve. Specifically, in the earlier stages of a technology there is a relatively higher degree of experimentation and learning involved that may have a dampening effect on recognized payoff. The focus of managerial attention at this point is not so much on maximizing payoff but the discretion to keep a technology "alive" with the knowledge that the steep part of the technology is the next stage. As the technology matures, the benefits derived from technologies begin to increase. This is reflected in the steep part of the technology curve. The focus of managerial attention at this point is on maximizing the payoff. After a certain stage along the continuum of technology maturity, there comes a time when it becomes necessary to jump the technology curve. Continuing with a technology that is past the steep part of the curve is a recipe for failure. The best technology managers are those who can let go of a technology, painful as that may be especially if it has yielded significant payoffs in the past, to jump onto a new technology that has its own technology curve. Therefore, at this point on the technology curve managerial focus is not on maximizing payoff from an existing technology but determining the optimal time and technology to jump. Thus, the position of a particular technology on the technology curve has significant implications for the payoff resulting, as well as what issues managerial attention should be targeting.

PAY ATTENTION TO S-CURVES OF NEW TECHNOLOGIES

The assessment and evaluation of new technologies, especially in the high technology industry, can be more complex than other forms of technology. By that, what we mean is that the payoff and performance of new technologies can actually be lower than the payoff and performance of technologies that they are meant to replace. However, this in and of itself should not be a reason for terminating a technology. Asthana[8] (1995)

---

8.   Praveen Asthana, "Jumping the Technology S-curve." *Chemtech,* October 1995.

cites the example of the magnetic 5-1/4 inch drives that replaced the 14-inch drives. When they were introduced, the 5-1/4 inch drives were in fact inferior (for instance, on density) and were not taken very seriously by the disk drive manufacturers. However, the technology was in the early, flat portion of the technology curve. It was allowed to survive and consequently improved at a pace fast enough to overtake the density of the 14-inch drive. The companies that prospered were the ones that were persistent with the technology and the 5-1/4 inch drives became the dominant technology.

BECOME COMFORTABLE WITH RENDERING YOUR PRODUCT OBSOLETE

Some of the most successful companies in the high technology arena have been those that have not hesitated in making their own products and technologies obsolete. The business adage that explains this phenomenon is "if you don't make your product obsolete then your competition will." Better you than your competition! If we get comfortable looking at technologies through the lens of the technology curve then we should be able to detect the maturity point at which the technology and its products might have to be rendered obsolete. Clinging to old technologies might seem the rational choice in the short run, but can be a threat to long-term competitiveness.

Two companies that are very adept at this strategy are Hewlett-Packard (HP) and Intel Corporation. HP introduced a new inkjet printer knowing full well that this would jeopardize sales of its laserjet printers. However, it went ahead with this technology because if HP didn't do it their competition would definitely introduce this technology and garner market share. Intel, on the other hand, introduces new 80x86 chips at such a fast pace that the competition has a difficult time keeping up with, let alone beating, Intel's technologies. HP and Intel are examples of two companies that never get too comfortable with their existing technology—they are always looking over their shoulders to make sure that the competition does not catch up.

This they do by jumping technology curves faster than their competition. The IT payoff approach will have to be adjusted accordingly. Normal rules of payoff will have to be suspended in the early stages of the S-curve. Perhaps an aggregate payoff analysis over the life cycle of the printer or computer chip is more likely to make a better case for investment.

RECOGNIZE COMPETITORS IN RELATED FIELDS

All too often, our view of competition has a narrow definition that is restricted to a certain industry. While we remain engrossed in what happens in our industry our radar may miss altogether what happens in a related industry that may have a significant effect on the success of the existing product or technology. For example,[9] IBM was so obsessed with competition from other mainframe manufacturers such as Fujitsu, Hitachi, and Digital that it missed the bus on RISC (reduced instruction set computing) workstations because these competitors were not seriously considering this technology. But the actual threat came from companies that did not even show up on IBM's radar, such as Sun Microsystems, that were betting everything on RISC chips.

REDUCE MARKET ACCEPTANCE TIME

Very similar to the technology curve for a specific technology is an S-curve for products, which marketing professionals believe explains the buying behavior of consumers: the market penetration curve. This describes the pattern in which a new technology penetrates a market. The earliest buyers are those that are enthusiastic about new technologies and would like to have the latest and newest technologies. Sales volumes are relatively low from this group (about 2.5%).[10] The earliest buyers are followed by the initial adopters who buy a technology because they see a potential for payoff and are willing to take a

---

9. T.R. Reid, *The Chip*. (New York: Simon and Schuster, 1984).
10. Ibid.

risk with the technology. Their numbers are also not very significant (about 14%). These two categories represent the early market penetration of a new technology. The majority of the buyers, however, wait until the technology has either proven to enhance payoff or has received good reviews. At this stage, sales accelerate for the product. Eventually, market penetration falls off after this technology is replaced by a more attractive alternative in the eyes of the customer. The market penetration curve trails the technology curve because of the time that it takes for the market to accept a product. The implication from these two curves is how we can reduce the gap between the technology curve and the market penetration curve. One way to approach this would be to create products that are more efficient but have the same feel as the products they replace. Since the learning involved is minimal, market acceptance will come much quicker. An example is a computer with more memory and a faster chip—both features are significant enhancements over earlier products but to the end-customer they provide the same feel. To reduce risk of the success of new technologies, it may be a good idea to reduce the gap between the technology curve and the market acceptance curve.

TECHNOLOGY TREND CURVES

An aspect that is related to the technology S-curve is the technology trend curve. This curve can help in providing guidance to the nature and extent of the various technology projects and technologies that a high-technology company should invest in. In other words, it presents a simple way of examining the portfolio of technology investments to provide a quick pulse of the company. The curve looks like the one presented in Figure 7.3. At any point in time, technologies can be characterized as trailing-edge, leading-edge, or bleeding-edge technologies.[11] Trailing-edge technologies are those that are generally older than 4–5 years and examples of such systems might be inven-

---

11. Andres Fortino, *www.techedcon.com*.

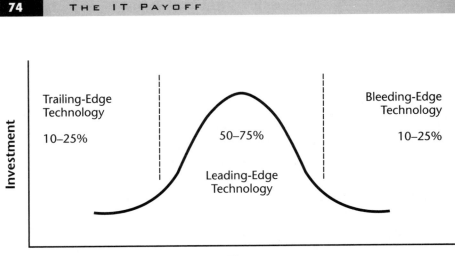

FIGURE 7.3 Technology trend curve.

tory systems and labor reporting systems. The technology is viable but may be expensive to maintain and modify. Generally, not more than 10%–25% of a business' technology should be in this category. Leading-edge technologies are those that are relatively new, 2–4 years. They offer the business a definite competitive advantage or allow a business to compete cost-effectively and help fulfill critical functions of the business. The majority of a business' technologies, between 50%–75%, need to fall under this category. Finally, bleeding-edge technologies are those technologies that are very new and in the developmental stages. While immediate benefits and payoffs accruing from these might not be very significant, they might be the technologies that ensure that the business survives in the future. Depending upon the type of industry and competition, about 10%–25% of the investment should be under this category. In summary, technology trends provide a way of assessing the portfolio of technology investments. They might serve as road maps, as businesses strive to move from their present position toward a desired technology trend curve or map them against an industry technology trend curve.

DISRUPTIVE TECHNOLOGIES

A recent business paradigm that is related to technology curves is the notion of disruptive technologies. Clayton Christensen's[12] work laid the foundation for viewing technologies through this framework. Much of the discussion in this section is condensed from the classic *Disruptive Technologies— Catching the Wave* by Bower and Christensen. Technological change is inevitable and when technologies or markets change, many leading companies fail to stay at the top of their industries due to the inability of company executives to foresee the impact of these changes and jump technology curves. This leads to loss of their leadership position and many times may also lead to their extinction. There are numerous examples of this phenomenon cited in the literature.[13] Xerox allowed Canon to define the small copier market. Goodyear entered the radial-tire market after their competition. A discernible pattern of failure is especially evident in the computer industry. Although IBM dominated the mainframe market, it missed the arrival of minicomputers by years. Digital Equipment was dominant in the minicomputer market but missed the personal computer market. Apple Computer was a leader in the personal computer market and the trendsetter for user-friendly computing, but fell behind in bringing its portable computer to market.

Companies that were once successful in the past fail because they succumb to one of the most popular and valuable management principals: staying close to their customers and aligning their investment in technologies to the needs of their customers. Paradoxical as this may seem, it is true. The large photocopying centers that formed a significant part of Xerox's original customer base had no use for small, slow tabletop copiers. In much the same way, IBM's large commercial and

---

12. Joseph L. Bower and Clayton M. Christensen, "Disruption Technologies—Catching the Wave," *Harvard Business Review,* January–February 1995.
13. Ibid.

governmental customers felt no need for minicomputers. These companies listened to their customers and were hurt by the very technologies their customers led them to ignore.[14]

The technological changes that drastically affect established companies are usually not completely new or complex from a *technological* perspective. But, they share two important characteristics: First, they typically present a novel package of attributes that at least initially are not valued by existing customers. Second, the attributes that existing customers do value improve at such a rapid pace that the new technology can invade established markets.[15] It is only at this point when mainstream customers desire that technology. Unfortunately for the established suppliers it is often too late: the innovators and owners of the new technology dominate the market.

Almost every industry has a critical performance criterion that is expected to improve over time. In photocopiers, an important performance measure is improvement in the number of copies per minute. In disk drives, one crucial measure is storage capacity. *Sustaining* technologies tend to maintain a rate of improvement. They give customers something better or more in the attributes they already value. *Disruptive* technologies, on the other hand, introduce a very different package of attributes from the one mainstream customers historically value. They also often perform far worse initially along one or two dimensions that are very important to those customers.

In evaluating proposed technological innovations, a company's revenue and cost structure play an important role. In general, disruptive technologies look financially unattractive to established companies. There is almost no market to research to see how profitable these technologies could be. There may be a need to change the structure of the company and, with emerging markets, established companies usually do

---

14. Joseph L. Bower and Clayton M. Christensen, "Disruption Technologies—Catching the Wave," *Harvard Business Review,* January–February 1995.
15. Ibid.

not want to risk what they already have. Once again, companies have to be aware that traditional rules of IT payoff assessment do not apply neatly here.

To overcome the impact of disruptive technologies, Bower and Christensen[16] propose several steps. The first step is to identify what constitutes a disruptive technology. One approach is to look at internal disagreements over the development of new products or technologies. Usually marketing and financial executives, because of financial incentives, will rarely support a disruptive technology. Top technical personnel, on the other hand, will often insist that a new market for the technology will emerge—even in the face of opposition from customers and marketing and financial staff. Disagreement between the two groups often signals a disruptive technology that senior managers should explore.

The next step is to define the strategic significance of disruptive technologies. If knowledgeable technologists believe the new technology might progress faster than the market's demand for performance improvement, then that technology, which may not meet customers' needs today, may very well address them tomorrow. Therefore, the new technology is strategically important.

The third step is to locate the initial market for disruptive technologies. Usually there is no existing market or basis against which to evaluate disruptive technologies. Managers need to create information about markets by finding answers to questions such as: Who will be the customers? Which attribute of product performance will matter to which customer? and, What will be the right price point? Managers can create this kind of information only by experimenting rapidly and inexpensively with both the product and market. For established companies to undertake such experiments is very difficult. It is best for them to let startups—either ones the company funds or others—conduct the experiments.

---

16. Joseph L. Bower and Clayton M. Christensen, "Disruption Technologies—Catching the Wave," *Harvard Business Review,* January–February 1995.

Established companies can also place responsibility for building a disruptive technology business in an independent organization. Creating a separate organization is necessary only when the disruptive technology has a lower profit margin than the mainstream business.

Disruptive technologies are part of a business unit's life cycle. The technological and market bases of any business will eventually disappear. Companies can be proactive and create new businesses to replace the ones that must eventually die. Managers of disruptive innovation must be empowered to realize the technology's full potential—even if it means an end to some of the mainstream business.

TECHNOLOGIES OF THE FUTURE

"I have a rule in my business: To see what happens in the next ten years, look at what happened in the last ten years."[17]

—ANDY GROVE, FORMER CEO OF INTEL CORPORATION

The words of wisdom from the former CEO of Intel suggest that the technology trends from the past can be a useful indicator of the technology trends of the future. In the context of technology curves, the underlying idea is to look at S-curves of technologies in the past and be able to make forecasts for the future.

As we look to the future, numerous promising technologies appear on the horizon: voice-enabled commerce (v-commerce), business-to-business collaborative technologies, mobile computing, biotechnologies. Where we are on the technology curves of these technologies might dictate significantly how much payoff we can derive from them. After assessing the maturity of the technologies in consideration, the next step will be to employ various tools to evaluate the technology, which are discussed in the following chapter.

17. Andy S. Grove, *Fortune*, ©1986. TIME, Inc. All rights reserved.

8

TECHNOLOGY
JUSTIFICATION
MODELS

Understanding the technology justification models can make the difference between anecdotal support and objective evidence of the business value of IT investment. Managers need to learn how to formulate business relationships into mathematical relationships and interpret findings resulting from quantitative models. Senior management is more likely to be persuaded to approve IT investment through scientifically sound analysis rather than political or perception means.

The purpose of the justification models is to convert the relationship between IT investment and anticipated payoff into a logical or mathematical form, while accounting for *other factors* that might affect the measurement along the way. Primarily, the objective of a model is to isolate the surplus profits that can be attributed to the investment. The complexity of these models increases as *other factors* are added on to either the cost or benefit side of the equation. In addition, certain justification models may be more appropriate given various organizational imperatives such as upgrading existing technology, investing in IT infrastructure, and acquiring new IT applications. Below we discuss various justification models such as intuition-based models, cost–benefit analyses, break-even point, net present value (NPV), economic value added (EVA), and regression-based statistical models.

Our experience indicates that often the payoff justification is driven by a desire to satisfy an internal relations need rather than any real concern for IT investment. The moment a request for productivity data comes in from the corporate office, IT managers hurry to gather project information from each subordinate so that they are prepared to justify the need for personnel in the department. In such cases, the "appearance" of IT stewardship is perhaps as critical as any objective payoff.

To cater to the "appearance" factor, focus groups consisting of a cross-section of client individuals can provide the public relations exposure as well as useful feedback of what they perceive as important. Focus groups can help guide the IT payoff process toward identifying the key variables that should be captured for costs as well as benefits. If the clients perceive an outcome from the technology to be important, however insignificant, that should be included in the benefits side of the equation. Nevertheless, as good stewards of corporate resources, managers should consider having a mechanism for ongoing data collection to evaluate the returns from IT investment.

Logical or intuition-based models represent the relationship between cost and benefit in a mathematical or graphical format and are widely used to examine the benefits from an investment as well as to determine the time to recoup the investment. Below we review an example of an IT investment and then examine how the various models can apply.

In one financial services company, the IT systems and the technical support structure were critical to respond to customer requests. Yet, almost every computer user in the company had experienced poor service from the office automation department. It was difficult to get someone from the computer department on the phone, complaint call tickets were misplaced, response time was routinely long, persons assigned to a support call were often not the right matches for the problem, and support staff gave different answers to the same problem.

The help desk consists of network-based software with a searchable database, along with a scheduling subsystem. The system also has the capability to reroute phone calls to anyone available on the support team. This is in contrast to the previous setup where one clerical person recorded the problem and assigned it to the technical support personnel. Now each member of the support team enters the problem call into the help desk system. Using the help desk database, the support team has loaded a number of common support issues that could be tracked and assigned to an appropriate support person. The system is accessible from any client location, and technicians can go from one service call to another without having to come back to the office to pick up service tickets. Problem resolutions are entered into the database remotely and are instantly available to all other support personnel. This enables consistent answers to other support problems as well as accurate troubleshooting. One year after the help-desk system was implemented most problems were resolved.

When it was announced at the semi-annual CIO Forum that the number of complaints had declined 40%, no one needed convincing. As the slide showing the decline appeared on the screen, there were many heads nodding among the audience. In a qualitative way, the investment in IT and the subsequent decline in complaints was already being validated through informal means. In such cases it may not be necessary to apply complex mathematical models to demonstrate payoff. Instead, a high-level cost–benefit analysis representing the costs and the resulting benefits from reduced calls, faster resolution time, fewer repeat calls, and so on, can suffice.

We are not advocating that the intuition-based models are a substitute for rigorous mathematical and statistical analysis. However, we are suggesting that in some cases it may not be necessary to convince the stakeholders that IT payoff has been achieved. Having said that, the intuition-based model does not preclude the quantification of the benefits, should that still be of interest. In the above help-desk situation, the decline in complaints and subsequent improvement in productivity can be calculated by multiplying the reduction in support time by an average wage rate. Once the total cost of the help-desk implementation is subtracted from the benefits, IT payoff is determined by the following equation:

IT payoff =
[Savings (in hours) for all problem resolution
× Average hourly wage rate]
– Cost of help desk implementation

Representing this relationship in a mathematical model, we get:

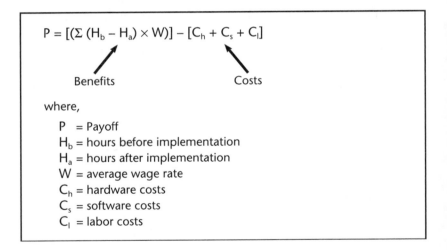

$$P = [(\Sigma (H_b - H_a) \times W)] - [C_h + C_s + C_l]$$

Benefits   Costs

where,

P = Payoff
H_b = hours before implementation
H_a = hours after implementation
W = average wage rate
C_h = hardware costs
C_s = software costs
C_l = labor costs

FIGURE 8.1 Cost–benefit analysis.

The formula in Figure 8.1 is a representation of a *cost–benefit analysis* that can be as simple as summing the total implementation costs from the general ledger and aggregating the total tangible benefits. Additional savings from the help desk can be added by accounting for quick troubleshooting, better customer service due to fewer downtime occurrences, and improved customer satisfaction and retention. Similarly, support staff training, system upgrades, and software maintenance can be accounted for as costs. Innovative use of historical data can further pay off if the company examines the common types of hardware problems and changes vendors or finds alternative hardware.

It should be noted that one could spend a lot of time identifying and gathering the costs and benefits of an implementation. After a certain point, the effort and time involved provides diminishing returns. Therefore, it is important to recognize when the cost of measurement begins to diminish the payoff being measured.

The cost–benefit approach is a practical approach for most situations, however, the depth of the analysis depends upon the demand for IT justification and other factors contributing to IT payoff. If there is no political or economic pressure to demonstrate a detailed payoff, there is no need to spend resources in doing so.

The *break-even point* (BEP) is generally used to identify the point at which the system investment has paid for itself. It may be used in situations where companies have to invest in a system that they perceive as not adding a great deal of value to the business but is the cost of doing business. For instance, when an automobile manufacturer mandates that in order for suppliers to continue to get business, they will have to implement electronic data interchange (EDI), the suppliers have to evaluate if they should invest in EDI or forego the customer. In such cases, the break-even point determines the point in the business relationship when the investment will have paid for itself.

A BEP is the same as cost–benefit analysis, when the cost = benefits or cost – benefits = 0. The *payback period* determines the duration of time in which the system is paying for itself. In other words, the duration of time during which the BEP is reached. Whereas the BEP may be expressed in units of service or parts, the payback period is expressed in units of time such as the number of weeks, months, or years.

Among the *other factors* we mentioned earlier is time. IT investments made today are not the same as IT investments made a year from today. Neither are dollars invested today the same as dollars invested a year from today. Why? In addition to the strategic head start, the present value of a dollar is greater than that of a dollar one year from today because the interest the dollar can gain or the returns on investment opportunity it presents. Therefore, the investment is required to generate positive return to break even. This "time value of money" is represented in an IT payoff measurement concept called net present value (NPV). How do we put a value on the time value on the money? The discount factor (DF) determines this. DF is the rate at which the company would have accumulated more money if it had not invested in the IT. This is based upon the interest rates and the returns from the stock market. Calculating the DF is usually the more challenging part because it requires experience and educated guesswork as to how the market will behave in the future (see Figure 8.2).

How can NPV help in measuring IT payoff? Recall from our earlier discussion that the investment in IT payoff competes with other investments such as manufacturing equipment, additional distribution centers, and advertising. Managers may examine the NPV value of continued investment in IT against that of other investments in determining the expected payoff and then decide which investment to make.

Year	Investment	Formula	Calculation	DF	PV
1	$2,500,000	$1/(1.15)^1$	1/1.15	0.869565	$2,173,913
2	$2,500,000	$1/(1.15)^2$	1/1.3225	0.756143667	$1,890,359
3	$2,500,000	$1/(1.15)^3$	1/1.520875	0.657516232	$1,643,791
4	$2,500,000	$1/(1.15)^4$	1/1.749006	0.571753246	$1,429,383
				2.854978145	**$7,137,445**

NPV

FIGURE 8.2 Calculation of NPV of the Help Desk investment.

In our Help Desk investment example, the financial services company can weigh the NPV value of IT against that of more advertising to solicit more business. Assume that the company will be spending $2.5 million a year for a period of 4 years, that is, $10 million to implement the system in all its divisions. The company can expect to earn about a 15% return by investing in advertising instead. Therefore, the discount factor is 0.15. The NPV is calculated in Figure 8.3.

In Figure 8.2, the column Year indicates the investment in each of the four years. For simplicity, we assume a $2.5 million investment in each year. The Formula and Calculation columns indicate the DF calculation for each year. For instance, given the 0.15 discount rate in the first year, the formula is $1/1.15$. In the second year it is $1/(1.15 \times 1.15)$ or $(1.15)^2$ while in the third year it is $1/(1.15 \times 1.15 \times 1.15)$, and so on. This yields

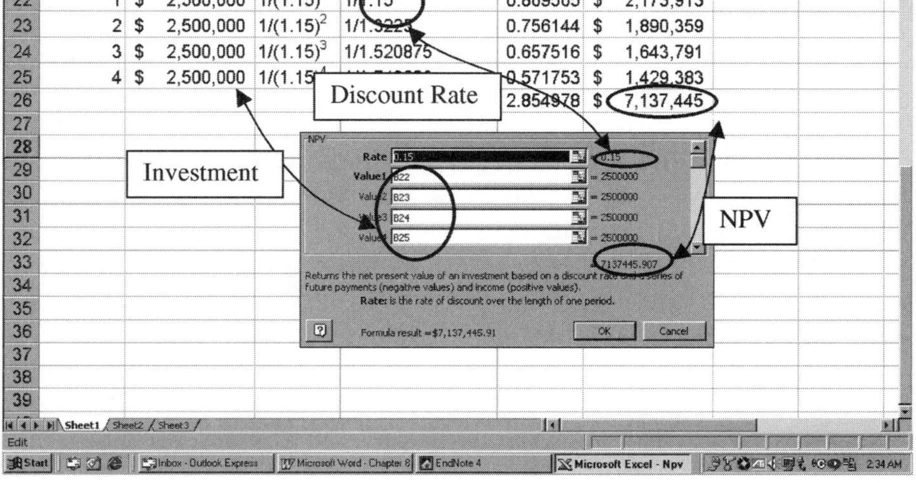

FIGURE 8.3 Calculation of NPV of Help Desk investment in Microsoft Excel.

the DF for each year. The DF multiplied by the investment for the year, that is $2.5 million, results in the present value (PV) for each year. The sum of all PVs is the NPV of the $10 million investment. In other words, if the payoff from Help Desk is less than $2,862,554 ($10,000,000 – $7,137,445), the company is better off investing in advertising.

As shown in Figure 8.3, the NPV calculation can also be accomplished efficiently in Microsoft Excel® or other spreadsheet software by using the financial function "NPV."

THE REAL OPTIONS APPROACH

While NPV provides information about the time value of the investment, it does not take into account the risks or opportunities created by stopping, decreasing, or increasing investment in the future. Investment in real-world scenarios is more complicated than a yes or no decision to invest or not to invest! Recall that in Figure 8.2, the investment is listed as $2.5 million in Years 2, 3, and 4. Given the additional information about how the Help Desk is perceived, the management has the option to increase or decrease investment any time after the first year.

Oftentimes it is worth the risk to continue investing, even if it is minimal, in IT initiatives because of the potential of a piece of the payoff pie in the future. Traditionally, these situations have challenged investors in Research and Development or high-risk ventures such as oil drilling. In the IT context, failure to make an investment in the network infrastructure, such as laying cable, can severely restrict a company's competitive capability to add computer applications and provide new services. Even when it is possible to retrofit infrastructure to adopt new applications, the valuable time lost in upgrading can put the company at a disadvantage. To deal with such future IT "options" that a business might have, an approach called Real Options is utilized.

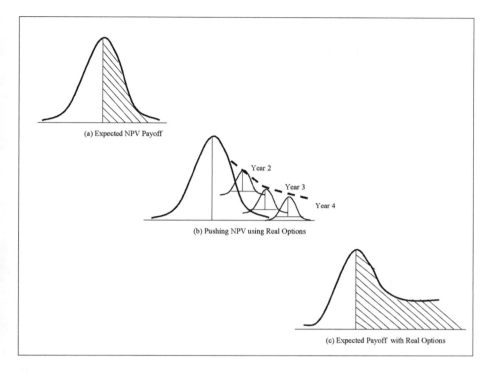

(a) Expected NPV Payoff

Year 2

Year 3

Year 4

(b) Pushing NPV using Real Options

(c) Expected Payoff with Real Options

FIGURE 8.4 Real Options compared with traditional NPV. Adapted from Flatto (1996).

Although the mathematical derivations and formula development of Real Options is beyond the scope of this book, we illustrate the concept in simple terms in Figure 8.4. Figure 8.4 (a) indicates the NPV concept, where the shaded area is the most likely NPV. The curve represents the likelihood of the value over the 4-year period of the investment. As indicated in Figure 8.4 (a), the curve assumes that once the decision to invest is made, it will continue to occur at the same pace for the next four years. The shaded area represents the likelihood of the expected payoff. We discussed above that it is not necessarily the case in the business world. Businesses do have the option to change the level of investment, redirect the efforts to support investment, or stop the investment. In effect, Figure 8.4 (b) shows just that. At each year starting the second year, the management can evaluate the IT investment payoff and set the future direction, in effect pushing the curve so that the opportunities are availed of and the risks mitigated. Figure 8.4 (c) indicates the revised shaded area using the Real Options approach. As is evident, pushing the curve out leads to an increased likelihood of achieving the expected payoff.[1] Yet, the key contribution of the Real Options approach is its ability to take advantage of unexpected or unforeseen opportunities. In simple terms, NPV is akin to a 30-year lease on a house, where rising inflation or greater demand for housing will not lead to rent increases. The Real Options approach would then be comparable to a 30-year lease where one has the option to renew the terms, sublease the property, end the lease in each year, or buy the property.

ECONOMIC VALUE ADDED

Economic value added (EVA) is defined as the return on invested capital, that is, after-tax cash flow generated by a company, minus the cost of the capital in creating the cash flow. Peter G. W. Keen[2] argues that the commonly used earnings per share tell us nothing about the cost of generating those profits. If the earnings per share are 10% and the cost of capital is 12%, it reduces rather than adds economic value. For IT payoff, EVA can serve as a complementary tool, when NPV and Real Options are being calculated by accounting for the cost of capital to assess the value of the investment.

STATISTICAL APPROACHES

While NPV and Real Options are financial approaches to modeling IT investment and expected payoff, statistical mod-

---

1. J. Flatto, "The Role of Real Options in Valuing Information Technology Projects," *Proceedings of the AIS conference*, Phoenix, AZ, August 16–19, 1996. *hsb.baylor.edu/ramsower/ais.ac.96/papers/FLATTO.htm*

2. Peter G.W. Keen, *The Process Edge: Creating Value Where It Counts.* (Boston: Harvard Business School Press, 1997).

els can also assist in finding and understanding the relationship between the investment and payoff. Most commonly, the first step is to examine the correlation table listing the strength of the relationship between the investment (independent) variables, and the payoff (dependent) variables. The following example of IT payoff data (Figure 8.5) shows expenditures in IT and profits for the organization. We then calculate the correlation coefficient in Excel. A perfect positive correlation is indicated by a coefficient of 1.0 and no correlation is indicated by a coefficient of 0.

The figure shows the CORREL function in Excel with a value of .74587. Since the correlation of 1.0 is a perfect relationship, this indicates a strong relationship between IT investment and payoff. Now that we know the relationship, it will be of interest to understand what contributes to the profitability besides the investment. After all, investment alone is

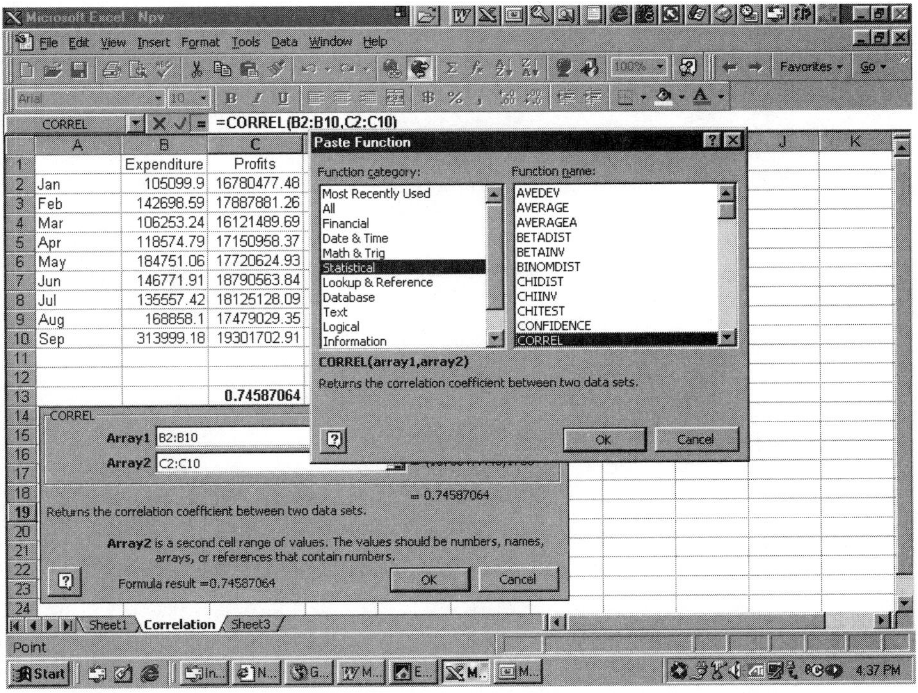

FIGURE 8.5 Excel screen of correlation analysis.

not sufficient. Based upon discussions with customers, we therefore might gather additional variables, such as (1) complexity of the workload (based upon the type of product mix) and (2) number of orders.

In the next level of payoff analysis, we study the extent of the contribution of each item to performance by constructing a regression equation. The regression equation can also be built in Excel, although more advanced functionality is available in statistical packages such as SPSS, SAS, and Minitab. The following screens (Figures 8.6 and 8.7) demonstrate how to execute a regression analysis and get results. In Excel, from the Tools menu, choose Data Analysis. Choosing Regression from the menu prompts the dialog box shown in Figure 8.6.

The Y range implies the performance variable (also known as the dependent variable), that is, the outcome of interest. In this case the outcome of interest is the variable Profits. The X

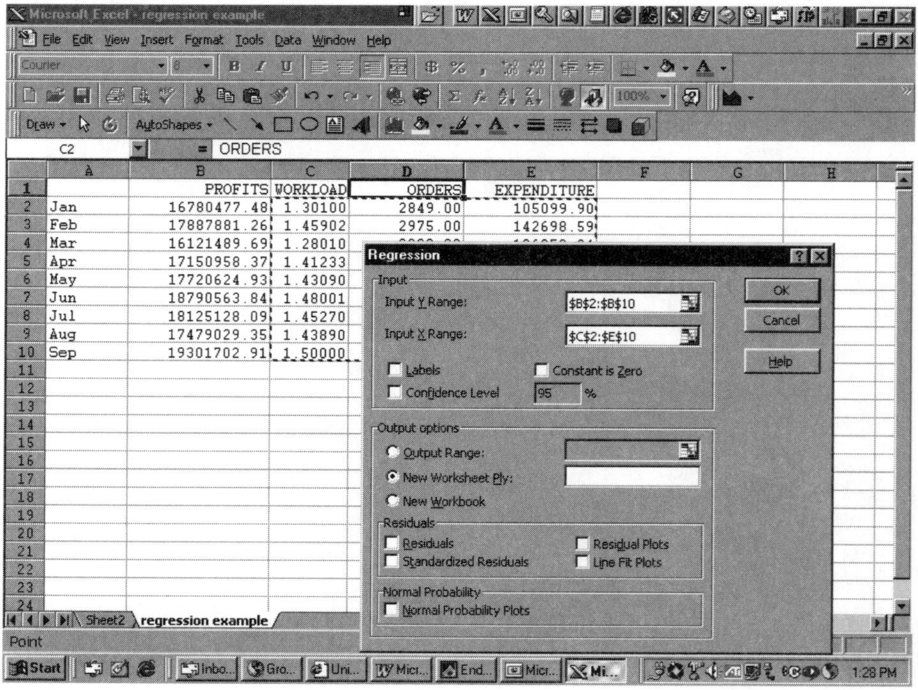

FIGURE 8.6 Excel screen of regression analysis.

range includes the variables that determine the value of the dependent variable (also known as the independent variables). In this case the independent variables are workload, orders, and expenditure. Simply stated, we are proposing that workload, number of orders, and IT expenditures determine the profits of the company.

The regression equation will convey the extent to which the variation in profit can be explained by workload, number of orders, and expenditures on IT through the reported statistic R-square. The Significance of F value will suggest if our proposed relationship is statistically valid. The coefficient and their corresponding *p* values will show the extent to which each independent variable contributes to determining profits and the confidence we can place in this determination.

The results of the regression analysis are shown in Figure 8.7. The Adjusted R-Squared (.96206) indicates that over 96%

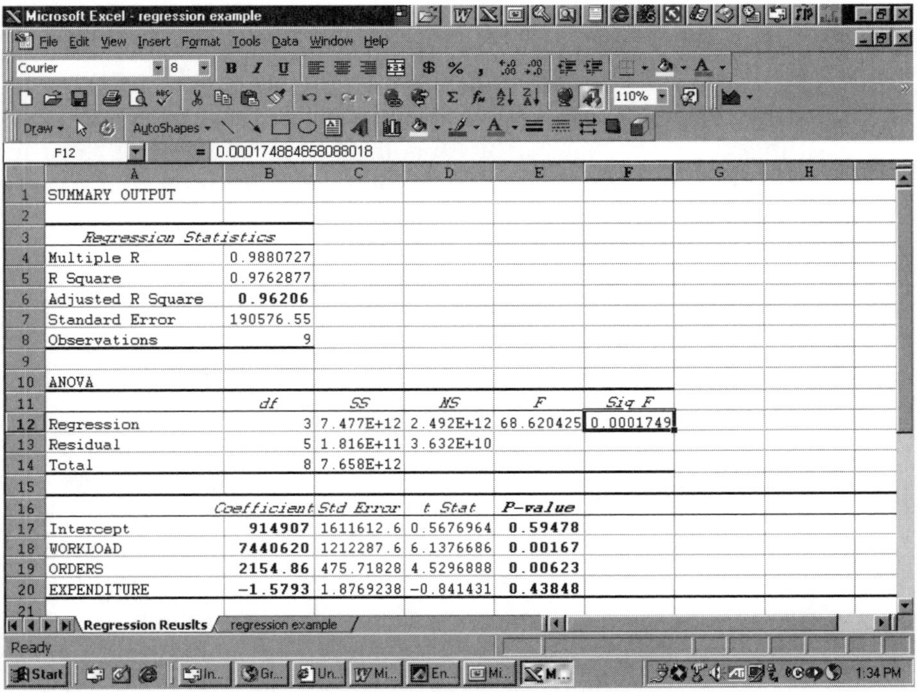

SUMMARY OUTPUT					
Regression Statistics					
Multiple R	0.9880727				
R Square	0.9762877				
Adjusted R Square	**0.96206**				
Standard Error	190576.55				
Observations	9				
ANOVA					
	df	*SS*	*MS*	*F*	*Sig F*
Regression	3	7.477E+12	2.492E+12	68.620425	0.0001749
Residual	5	1.816E+11	3.632E+10		
Total	8	7.658E+12			
	Coefficient	*Std Error*	*t Stat*	***P-value***	
Intercept	**914907**	1611612.6	0.5676964	**0.59478**	
WORKLOAD	**7440620**	1212287.6	6.1376686	**0.00167**	
ORDERS	**2154.86**	475.71828	4.5296888	**0.00623**	
EXPENDITURE	**−1.5793**	1.8769238	−0.841431	**0.43848**	

FIGURE 8.7 Excel results of regression analysis.

of the variation in profits is explained by workload, number of orders, and expenditures on IT. Sig F (.0001749) indicates that there is less than 1 in 1,000 chance that there might be no relationship between the three independent variables and profit.

The coefficients indicate that if the workload increases by 1 unit, the profitability will increase by $7,440,620 (p = .00167). Although this appears to be a large number, it seems reasonable because the workload data indicates that increases are in decimal points as opposed to units. Similarly, each additional order is likely to increase the profits by $2,154 (p = .00623). In both these cases we conclude an increase because the coefficients are positive. However, this is not the case for Expenditure, the coefficient for which is −1.5793, that is, for $1.00 of expenditure (IT investment), the company can expect approximately $1.58 decline in profits. The p value (.438) of the expenditure coefficient indicates that our results might be indicative of no relationship between expenditure and profits 44 times out of 100.

Overall, from the above analysis we can conclude that there is evidence that the three independent variables—workload, orders, and expenditure—determine profit. Next, we are quite confident that workload and number of orders affect the level of profits. We are not confident in our findings of the relationship between expenses to profits. Moreover, the negative relationship is somewhat counterintuitive.

In spite of the above counterintuitive results, such findings are not unusual. First, a quick observation of the data set indicates that the sample size is not enough. Even a moderate variation in profits can be exaggerated in a 9-month data set. Second, lag effects of investment are not accounted for in the data. Expenditures and profits data are for the same month. To be accurate, expenditure of a given month should be matched with profitability of some future month. This lag is important for the expenditure to create the relevant IT assets, the IT assets to create the impacts, and these impacts to appear in the company's balance sheet. Clearly, the time for lag effects to appear will vary among various organizations and technologies. Statistical software packages such as SPSS and SAS provide a "lag" function that can be used in developing a regression model. While using an Excel spreadsheet, an artificial lag effect can be created by staggering the performance data by one or more periods. This can be accomplished easily by creating a column, Jan1, and copying the data from the January column. Similarly, the same can be done for other periods.

Third, examination of expenditure data may reveal that some expenditure was not directly related to the payoff under study. For example, expenditure for the month of September of $313,999.18 as compared to other months appears suspect. It is possible that it was for a one-time expense such as annual licensing or maintenance, thereby artificially inflating the expenditure for the month.

Even if the expenses correspond to IT investment, the absence of profit data for the succeeding month makes it difficult to evaluate the impact of this expenditure on profitability. In this case, the September data is an outlier and perhaps be excluded from the analysis. Finally, the analyst should consider gathering data for additional variables that might better explain the IT payoff. As proposed earlier, this search for additional variables should include intermediate variables alongside profit, such as reduction in transportation costs as a result of an EDI implementation, reduction in accounts receivable days for an ERP system, or concept-to-market days for a CAD/CAM system.

Technology justification models form the basis of quantitatively expressing the expected value of IT investment. However, the justification approach is likely to succeed only when utilized as part of a larger approach for assessing the implementation of an IT payoff. The next chapter presents such an approach to institute a process in an organization.

9

IMPLEMENTING
IT PAYOFF
INITIATIVES:
A FRAMEWORK

All too often companies realize the need for measuring payoff when it is already too late to measure. The need may arise when board members question the CEO or CIO on the value of certain initiatives. Other times it is felt when the talk around the water cooler is about how much money the company is "wasting" on these computer projects while employees are being laid off. We have seen "Monday morning quarterbacking" in the hallways soon after a new ERP system is implemented such as: "What have we gained by spending $13 million, and who knows how much we are spending on those high-paid consultants, when the new system does the same things as the old system."

This is when IT managers and functional managers who initiated the projects start gathering quantitative evidence that the investment indeed pays off. To some business customers, IT is the cost of doing business and therefore IT spending is a black box. Even when people understand that IT pays off, they have different ideas about how payoff should manifest itself. Some expect to see faster access to information, others expect an upgrade to their desktop systems, and some count on the system to never hang up in the middle of a transaction. While expectations may vary from being realistic and achievable to being completely unrealistic, what is real is that these expectations have to be managed. An IT payoff analysis on the benefits of IT payoff is needed before such questions are raised. The IT department should incorporate assessment and measurement into IT spending plans while being vigilant of such perceptions.

It is clear that measuring and selling the value created by IT should be managed as a subproject. Many organizations have trouble getting started and have difficulty deciding where to begin the measurement process. This is understandable given that the measurement process is a complex one and depends upon various contextual factors. To simplify how to implement the IT payoff measurement initiatives, Figure 9.1

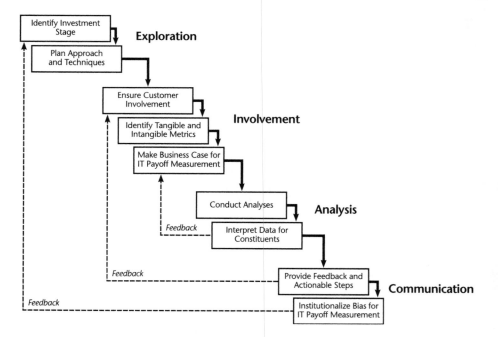

FIGURE 9.1   The 4-phase EIAC model for instituting IT payoff initiatives.

outlines our four-phase approach—exploration, involvement, analysis, and communication (EIAC)—to institute and measure IT payoff. Each phase consists of several substeps, described in greater detail in the following sections.

PHASE I: EXPLORATION

The exploration phase has two purposes: (1) to develop a basic understanding of what is to be measured depending upon the company's stage of investment, and (2) the approach taken to analyze the data matched with the analytical technique. IT investment can be influenced by the stages of investment, for example, whether the investment is strategic or operational, or if the technology is a breakthrough or an upgrade to an existing technology. This phase is a reality check of the opportunities created by the investment in IT and its market positioning to exploit such opportunities. Porter's two strategic frameworks (Chapter 3) can assist in this assessment.

Identify investment stage. An example of the stage of IT lifecycle in the organization is its investment in the infrastructure. The infrastructure investment of a new organization is likely to be measured differently than an investment in upgrading legacy systems to Web-based technologies. Infrastructure investments payoff, over a longer term, generally manifest through other IT investments and therefore is difficult to measure. Legacy systems have a history of outcomes and can be easier to measure. Furthermore, each type of investment will have different expectations from their respective user base and will be governed by significantly different metrics. It is important to assess the stage because it points us to the relevant metrics. One or more of several approaches can support various steps of the project and techniques to ensure that appropriate payoff metrics are identified, measured, and communicated.

Plan approach and techniques. An investment in an upgrade of the existing infrastructure can be measured through net present value of the total investment. For instance, if the IT investment involves upgrading the email and scheduling system, the investment is generally approved at one time and involves several stages of deployment, such as the upgrade of the operating system, additional data storage capacity, and training. NPV can be utilized to calculate the real cost in today's dollars after the implementation is complete.

Infrastructure investment can be in high-risk opportunities, for example, implementation of an integrated ERP system by a pharmaceutical manufacturer in preparation for the impending expansion of a retail pharmacy chain customer. In the event that the retail drug chain fails in implementing the enterprise-wide ERP system, it constitutes a high risk. Yet, there are other opportunities the manufacturer can seek to collaborate with other retail chains or its own suppliers. In doing so, it can improve its own operations through better forecasting and planning capabilities afforded by the ERP system. These opportunities (or risks) of the investment stage can be explored and exploited at each stage of the investment as the project proceeds from Year 1 to Year 2, from Year 2 to Year 3, and so on, by matching it with an appropriate technique.

Frito Lay Inc., the leading snack foods manufacturer, implemented a handheld computer system that initially saved several hours a week of delivery persons' time in completing paperwork. However, as the implementation progressed, additional advantages of continued investment became clear and the company began to use daily sales data to plan production, forecast sales, track the effects of promotional campaigns, and eventually plan organizational redesign.

In both cases the Real Options approach is appropriate in identifying future risks and opportunities when the IT investment should be curtailed, stopped, or continued. It provides advantages over NPV because the late-stage benefits would not have been envisioned prior to the investment, thereby resulting in an understatement of payoff.

PHASE II: INVOLVEMENT

This phase addresses organizational issues more than the technical or analytical aspects of IT payoff. More precisely, it has to do with involving the stakeholders in an attempt to thwart what could become a political issue. It is often argued that the most common reason for IT failure is managerial, not technical. Often the reasons for failure come down to hurting people's feelings because either they were not consulted prior to an announcement or not asked to provide feedback on how to proceed. There is a tendency to resist or oppose an initiative following such overlooked communication. Second, a pragmatic reason for involvement is determining how the payoff will be measured and utilized by the company. After all, it is the customers who will implement changes resulting from IT payoff analysis and it makes sense to involve them as much as possible.

Ensure customer involvement. If we are going to measure the business value of IT investment, it is critical to involve the businesspeople in agreeing upon what is to be measured. Jim Elert, Chief Information Officer for Trinity Health, suggests that "IT should enter into a negotiation with the business side of the company on what constitutes value and how it will measured." If this agreement is not secured ahead of time, there is the possibility of faultfinding with the IT payoff assessment, particularly if the results do not favor a customer's agenda. Customers also provide access to performance data necessary to conduct the analysis. Although the expense data are available in the accounting department, the performance metrics generally reside at the operational departments under the customers' control. Without customer involvement, identifying appropriate metrics and making the business case will be difficult.

Identify tangible and intangible metrics. Involving the constituents helps identify those metrics that are important to them. Metrics can take the shape of measuring something as straightforward as the time it takes to execute a customer service call or to fill an order. However, the intangible metrics can be hard to identify, let alone measure. For instance, an increase in market share, reduction in customer complaints, or reduced reject rate could be difficult to place a value upon. Under some circumstances, increasing market share could mean that the company is getting customers that the competition does not want. The reduction in customer complaints could mean that dissatisfied customers are not speaking up because they chose not to come back. Similarly, reduced reject rate could mean that more defective parts are getting through. With the involvement of the customers, appropriate metrics can be identified and agreed upon so that an acceptable analysis can be accomplished.

Make the business case for IT payoff measurement. One of the most challenging issues in IT payoff is demonstrating to the organization that it is worth the company's time and expense to conduct the analysis. We have encountered various questions from concerned employees on the objective of measuring IT payoff because they are skeptical of the organization's motives. They are concerned about whether the IT payoff exercise is really a productivity assessment to see if certain functions are paying off. Such concerns take the form of rumors such as that a department is a candidate for shutting down or outsourcing if it does not show IT payoff. On the other end of the spectrum is the argument that "the company is doing well financially so we must be doing something right. Why waste time in measuring IT payoff?"

In some cases this is a reasonable question. Why take away resources from doing the work when there are no problems? It is widely known that any measurement attempt, particularly one that involves measuring people performance, is likely to disturb the system. Therefore, it is imperative to make the case for measuring IT payoff and convince the entire organization of its value. The payoff measurement areas should be clearly outlined, the measures agreed upon, and the actions expected as a result of the findings should be understood. Management should clearly state how actions taken would result in organizational improvements such as better working conditions, increased competitiveness, further investment, or redesigned processes. In some cases it is simple to make the business case when the IT payoff is needed to report to a governmental or trade agency. The business case for IT payoff measurement is easier to make if the company is feeling the "pain," such as in a general dissatisfaction with information systems, threat of loss of market share, customer complaints, or a difficult choice of investing in IT or other initiatives. Relating payoff measurement to these reasons can help employees understand and subsequently offer buy-in to the project.

PHASE III: ANALYSIS

In the analysis phase, data are collected, analyzed, and interpreted for meaningful action. Notice that this is the third phase of the IT payoff measurement process. We draw attention to this fact because we find IT payoff analysts leaping to data collection and analysis without spending adequate time in the exploration and involvement phases. It is not a coincidence that the technology justification models are in the second half of this book. The analysis phase is preceded by significant preparation, careful attention to which is likely to be rewarded by accurate results that customers will accept and act upon. It is this "fit" between the measurement approach and organizational goals that one should seek to accomplish.

Conduct analysis. The analyst should choose from the various techniques mentioned in the earlier chapters and find one or more that are suitable to the objectives of the customers. Of course the availability of data also dictates the use of analytical tools. The prevailing issues in conducting IT payoff analysis are lag effects, control variables, and adjustment factor.

The lack of longitudinal data has been a major shortcoming of several past IT payoff studies. Longitudinal data for the same metrics over an extended number of periods allow the analysis to account for lag effects in IT payoff. IT investment made today is likely to take one or two quarters before the company can expect a payoff.

Isolating the effects of technology from other causes that can affect financial performance have challenged analysts and led customers to be skeptical. The company's performance can be affected in part by a recession or a growing economy, higher raw material prices, or redesigned business processes. To account for such confounding factors, the analysts gather additional data to account for hypothesized factors included in the analysis as control variables. Such factors should be identified in the Involvement phase while working with the customers. Regression analysis can identify the "interaction effect" in isolating effects of IT. A recent study analysis compared the effect of IT investment with that combined with business process reengineering initiatives, also known as *interaction effect*. The study found that although there was evidence of IT payoff resulting from investment, the payoff was more pronounced when combined with business process reengineering.[1]

While discussing the NPV, we discussed that investment made today does not have the same value of investment made at a later date because of the time value of money. Similarly, the value of technology also changes over time. Per Moore's law, within two years the performance of computer hardware will probably double for the same price or cost half as much for the same performance. Therefore, to account for these variations, analysts use an adjustment factor to discount future investment so that a fair comparison can be made.

Interpret data for constituents. The results of a statistical analysis have little meaning if they are not translated into business terms. A regression equation with a set of coefficient values has turned off many customers who believe that the complex analysis is an academic exercise. Therefore, the results of the analysis should be validated for reasonableness and translated into business terms. In a real-life business situation, a consulting company was given the responsibility of conducting a payoff analysis of the customer satisfaction tracking system. Following rigorous statistical analysis when

---

1.   S. Devaraj and R. Kohli, "Information Technology Payoff in the Healthcare Industry: A Longitudinal Study," *Journal of Management Information Systems, 16* (2000): 39–64.

the results were presented, the customers' reaction was subdued. The reason: the results of the analysis were common knowledge and therefore the business case for the analysis could not be made. Although upon further analysis, interesting drivers of customer satisfaction and potential contribution of the system to the organization were uncovered, and this was only after the consultants worked with the sponsors of the initiative to identify metrics that were meaningful to the end-customers. As indicated in Figure 9.1, a feedback loop leading to the previous phase is recommended so that the customers' help is sought to establish the business value of the analysis and interpretation of meaningful results.

Typically, the results of the analyses are first presented to the sponsors of the IT payoff initiative in a report or a presentation prior to dissemination to the entire end-customer base (discussed later). The sponsors are generally interested in the relationship of IT investment with the resulting benefits. Some questions the data interpretation should address are:

1. Is IT investment paying off?
2. If so, what is the extent of the payoff? If none, why?
3. How much increased revenue or profit can be attributed to a unit amount invested, for example, in the ERP system?
4. Are some investments paying off more than other investments? Why or why not?
5. What are the factors that facilitate/inhibit payoff?
6. Is continued IT investment recommended?

Careful analysis and interpretation of data to answer these questions is likely to win approval for continuation of the project and wider implementation of the findings.

PHASE IV: COMMUNICATION

The communication phase can appear to some as intuitive or even redundant. However, the fact is that most initiatives fail to have the desired effect because of lack of timely, complete, and meaningful communication. It is a thankless job and perhaps noticed only when not done properly. Yet, it remains the cornerstone of getting people involved in organizational initiatives. An indicator of good communication is when constituents see the value of measurement of IT payoff and make it a part of the work plans.

Provide feedback and actionable steps. In the IT payoff context, the communication of the findings should be useful to the customer. The customers feel a part of the process and perceive getting something in return for sharing the data. This step is a continuation of the last step of the analysis phase—interpret data for constituents. In this step the findings of the analysis are broken down by functional areas and communicated appropriately. The analysis results have greater use when accompanied by actionable steps.

Analysts find this transition from results to actionable steps as the most challenging. It requires customization for each functional area and a deep understanding of the nature of the business, as well as some creativity in suggesting innovative ways to exploit payoff. Unless the results can be tied to day-to-day activities, profound changes are difficult to make. One may compare this step with customer "hand-holding"— and it may be just that. Yet it is necessary to close the loop of the IT investment to payoff. As discussed in Chapter 5, this is where IT assets will show impacts and these are the constituents who will enable such impacts. Without IT impacts, there will be no organizational impacts. The importance of customer involvement is depicted in a feedback loop to the beginning of the involvement phase. The analysts will be expected to show how the recommended actionable items will affect the metrics and support the business case for institutionalizing the IT payoff process.

Institutionalize bias for IT payoff measurement. Performance measurement is critical to organization success because of the reasoning that what you cannot measure, you cannot improve. In this final step of the final phase, we recommend that payoff measurement should become a bias within the organization. The payoff exercise should lead people to think of their work in measurement terms and encourage them to ask questions such as: Do we have the data to know that the technology investment does what it is supposed to do? How do we collect this data? What can it inform us?

The measurement bias should also be reflected in the technologies themselves. For instance, the company should implement ERP modules to track systems features accessed and overall usage, and relate the data to functional performance metrics. If managers use the corporate decision support system's (DSS) "what if" analysis to analyze contracting options, the longevity and profitability of contracts can be tracked to evaluate the DSS investment payoff. In our discussions with ERP managers, we find that such measurement modules, although available, are not utilized because of the overhead in capturing, storing, and processing large volumes of data. For quantifiable metrics, the implementation and enhancement of such tools are critical in creating a system where the data collection and analysis are continuous and proactive. The results of payoff analysis can be displayed on a corporate electronic dashboard alongside indicators of financial and quality performance that managers periodically monitor. Thus, the payoff analysis can be part of a balanced scorecard approach that was described earlier.

It is likely that some time in the future the indicators will generate the need for instituting another payoff analysis—perhaps in a new technology or a reengineered process. This will lead to a feedback loop to the beginning of the EIAC model and trigger another IT payoff measurement project (see Figure 9.1). However, this time the company will be better positioned to build upon the learning transpired from the erstwhile IT payoff. Furthermore, the measurement system in place might not require much modification, if any. In this respect, the EIAC model represents a life-cycle approach for IT investment and payoff measurement.

The four-phase EIAC approach described above is by no means an exhaustive one. Due to the nature of the business, one may add more steps or combine two or more steps. Furthermore, the time and effort spent on a step can vary depending upon the stage of the IT investment, past experience with measuring payoff, and the maturity of analytical tools within the organization. Nevertheless, the steps described in the EIAC approach should help in identifying gaps in the payoff measurement process to avoid some common pitfalls.

INTERVIEW WITH CINDA HALLMAN, PRESIDENT AND CEO, SPHERION CORPORATION

In your opinion, how is IT payoff measured among manufacturing organizations?

Cinda Hallman (CH): Most businesses do not adequately measure the benefits side or the payoff side of IT. They normally measure the cost side very well and have gotten much better at it. However, the problem is when you only measure the cost side, then IT becomes thought of as a cost, an overhead, as opposed to a component of doing good business. The IT payoff is in a lot of cases very difficult to measure but not impossible. At DuPont we had many very large projects, including a multimillion dollar SAP project. The measurement for this project was in and around what it could deliver in specific areas to the businesses as well as horizontally across all of our businesses. Procurement savings was the most substantial part of the payoff. The benefit was that the value of the information we gained enabled our buyers to leverage the buying capability for things, such as Maintenance Repair Operation (MRO) items,[a] which was quite substantial because in a company with 80 businesses, without this information it's difficult to grasp the leverage you may have in working with vendors.

What challenges does such measurement pose?

CH: With MRO items one has to have a tracking mechanism to ensure that the benefits in procurement are realized. To a large degree, businesses in the past have not had either a way of identifying the benefits, or if they did have a way of identifying the benefits in the business case they did not have a way of following up on it afterward to make sure that the benefits were actually realized. So that second part is a very important part of the puzzle and actually it turns out to be a part of the managing process within a company.

a. *MRO includes thousands of small items that are purchased in manufacturing operations ranging from safety gloves to safety shoes to gaskets to screws. For large companies MRO items add up to billions of dollars.*

If you don't have a measurement mechanism in the feedback loop, then in effect what will happen is an IT project will get implemented and there will never be any accountability on the benefit side, so in this regard IT projects have to be a part of the managing process and have to be treated like other projects within a company. Most substantial manufacturing companies have big engineering projects that have traditionally been measured from both the cost and benefits side.

How did you deal with such challenges?

CH: At Dupont I tried to use the practices that had been adhered to for engineering projects in that particular area as a way of illustrating to people what needed to be done in the IT area because they were quite familiar with these practices for measuring cost and benefit. That turned out to be a fairly good way of helping people to realize that measuring both cost and benefit needs to be a part of the managing process. It helps if the executive level in a company realizes that you need both the costs picture and the benefits picture too. If they seem to consider IT as just an overhead and only ask about the cost side of the equation, it makes it more difficult. So that's another component of achieving success in this arena.

How does measurement of investment in e-business opportunities differ from traditional IT investment?

CH: Among the projects that were more difficult to assess in terms of the benefit side included those that involved e-business work at DuPont. For newer applications, measuring payoff involves making the case that the company needs to get into this particular arena for a variety of reasons, either as a "stay-in-business" case, which could be true in some particular areas, or it could be a way that is going to help you with your cost provisions, which is certainly true in some areas because if done appropriately it streamlines the process or because you want to experiment. All of these actually are quite valid reasons to invest in e-business technologies. The payoff has to be tied to a leader of that particular business accepting responsibility that they want to experiment, that they want to try something, or that they believe that it is a price of staying in business. They have to be prepared to take accountability for helping the investment succeed. We were most successful in instances where the head of the business was committed to this.

Another ingredient of success is to try to ensure that you have provided as much education as possible to the business leader so they have some understanding of the area they are embarking on. We worked with an external supplier to set up workshops where they gathered information on one of our business areas all the way from the nylon business to the Lycra business to the engineering polymers to the various electronics businesses at DuPont. We then took the business leader along so that at the workshop the business leader was educated in a way of showing him or her about what was happening in their particular lines of business. They would be exposed to what their competitors were doing in the "e-arena" and then what was possible in this area. That was a tremendous help because it gave them more energy, a better understanding, and an appreciation of what others were doing. Therefore, it provided a nice balancing ground to move this thing forward. But the point again on payoff is that these particular kinds of areas are built around trust and judgment. Good business judgment means that "I know I've got to do something" and the trust is that "I am working with my colleagues in IT and other areas in the company in order to get the job accomplished and I know that my colleagues are going to get me the right kind of competency to get this thing done."

You have to structure the project so you share accountability for its success with the business leader. If you are talking about changing the way you do business, it could take a period of a year, if not longer, in order to transform the way you work. This makes it difficult to measure results. The best business leaders will measure results because they want to stop these things that are experiments. If the project doesn't look like it's returning something to you they will stop it. In most cases people that have helped start something find it difficult to stop it, but the strongest business leaders take a critical look at some of the areas that they were expecting to either improve; that is, by getting new business, different customers, more volume from existing customers, and perhaps cost reduction. If none of these are occurring on a minimal scale they will step back from it and consider whether they should proceed with the project. Some did and that shows that they understand good business. At the end of the day all IT projects are supposed to make the businesses better.

**INTERVIEW WITH CINDA HALLMAN,
PRESIDENT AND CEO, SPHERION CORPORATION**

You mentioned that the good ones would try to measure, but did you find that this impedes the productivity? Did the impetus for measurement of payoff come from the IT group or did it come from the business group?

CH: I think that it varies by individuals. To some extent it is driven by IT. I also think that IT people are trained to a large extent to work with the businesses on what they believe the businesses desire and so they can be influenced if a business leader doesn't want to measure. The person that you want to try to get in the right place the earliest is the business leader.

The question pertains to who is answerable to the senior management, who actually writes the check for the new project.

CH: Well the way it works in reality is sometimes different than how most people think it works. In a lot of cases, and all the cases I have been involved in, the head of IT has a pretty large share of the responsibility for what's done at IT and the company and they are expected to help steer the ship in the right direction. Now, what needs to occur is that the business leaders need to take more ownership for the benefits side. Again, in a lot of companies, the benefits side has been overlooked so all you're looking at is the cost side. Therefore, the IT person in many cases is held largely accountable in the company. What we were trying to move toward at DuPont is more accountability to the businesses for making the right decisions on these projects consistent with what they were trying to achieve in that business.

Was there a process laid out on how an investment is going to be made, at what point it is going to be measured and who was going to measure it, and how we are going to declare success or failure?

CH: We set up a process within IT where we placed what I would call "smaller CIOs" in some of the big businesses such as our Lycra business and our Nylon business. Those businesses were set up in a wide variety of ways. We had smaller CIOs within the business and those people had accountability for understanding that business area as well as understanding IT. It worked better if you can consider the CIO at the center of the wheel and the spokes running from the center into the businesses. Those people were accountable for working with the business leaders on projects and identifying appropriate projects consistent with the businesses' work plan. From a managing process standpoint, that's the way it works. The CEO was always looking to me (the CIO) to make sure that we were making the overall investment and directing it to help businesses understand where they should spend money in the most appropriate way. Our "smaller CIOs," working with the business leaders, were accountable to identify with the business leadership the benefits side and ensure that this was accounted for and followed up on. And so they were to a large extent helping to steer the investment in the right direction. We were on the road to some changes. Our people were smart enough to understand that this was just a way of getting them to improve their business and that IT was a critical tool and that they needed to measure it.

How would you contrast between your experiences in the manufacturing sector and now at the reigns of a services company? Do you see any new challenges or differences in the way IT payoff is approached or the metrics?

CH: Yes, I think that there are a tremendous number of similarities in the services industry. What I do find in the services industry is more need for "up-to-the-minute" information on certain things. However, in terms of the way projects are identified and prioritized and then benefits are assessed, there are very similar kinds of issues. And we also have multiple businesses within the services company that have the same kind of competing needs as well as resources that are not always equal to the demands. So we have the priority-setting problem, the competing challenges that one has to deal with and just like in a manufacturing company like DuPont, we have to get the infrastructure or the foundation systems in place while at the same time fulfill business unit demands. In addition, most businesses can easily see the benefit of Web-enablement because it looks attractive and glamorous and not realize the benefits of the infrastructure work that has to be in place to enable the front-end work.

Was there a difference in how you measured infrastructure versus an application such as the one that you described for the MRO application?

CH: The infrastructure work is usually quite large in terms of the expenditure and so one must be disciplined in measuring the benefits, and both the costs and the benefits, which is also usually a large number. In terms of the front-end work, in some cases those are entirely small projects and you don't want to put in place such a laborious measurement procedure that it makes it cumbersome and does not add value. We have a much slimmer process for small projects. It just wouldn't make sense to go through that laborious measurement procedure for these smaller projects. In certain cases there are things that either the CIO determines for the business or the business has an idea on what might help a customer for which you will do a short experiment. Again, you don't want long, laborious measurement procedures to stand in the way of something like that.

Are today's e-commerce technologies making it easier to measure payoffs?

CH: I don't see much difference. I think that the biggest opportunity area you still have in terms of the benefits is the very large infrastructure projects. I do think that with the pervasiveness of technology, which Web-enabled has made more widespread, we have to just accept the fact that technology is pervasive. Whereas in the old days we had cost justifications around a PC, today the PC has become the calculator. And so in effect you have to move up a step and say a PC is basic equipment for employees today. It is definitely different within my lifespan of being in IT and so I think that we have to accept those kinds of things for which one doesn't need to have cost justification.

Did you have accountants or consultants helping you with projected payoffs for large infrastructure investments for which detailed payoff or potential payoff analysis is needed?

CH: Well, within DuPont of course we have a very fine finance department and we always had people assigned from the finance/accounting area on these projects. They were assigned from a functional standpoint but they were also assigned to work on the business case as well. That is just standard practice. In certain cases we also got auditors involved early. It depended on the project and we certainly had other functional people that were relevant to the area. For example, it wasn't unusual when we were dealing on these large projects to have the legal department involved as well.

Cinda A. Hallman is the President and CEO of Spherion Corporation, a company that specializes in recruitment, outsourcing, and technology services. Prior to Spherion, Cinda served in a number of key senior executive roles during a more than 20-year career at DuPont (E.I. du Pont de

INTERVIEW WITH CINDA HALLMAN, PRESIDENT AND CEO, SPHERION CORPORATION

Nemours and Company). In her most recent role as Senior Vice President, DuPont Global Systems and Processes, Cinda led a major effort to define the new business models associated with transforming DuPont from a chemicals and energy-based company to a chemicals, biology, and knowledge-based company. She was also responsible for global information technology, processes, and strategy.

10 ELECTRONIC COMMERCE: CHALLENGES AND OPPORTUNITIES IN ASSESSING IT PAYOFF

The basic model presented in Chapter 9 is applicable to all technology investment contexts, including electronic commerce, or e-commerce. Yet, there are nuances in e-commerce that deserve further attention. This chapter addresses the challenging task of technology evaluation in predominantly Web-based environments. Specifically, it presents a framework that can be used to determine the various kinds of payoff metrics in e-commerce. Below, we discuss some recent business capabilities accelerated by the advent of e-commerce. Businesses investing in IT should develop and exploit these capabilities to enhance IT payoff.

DATA, INFORMATION, AND KNOWLEDGE

One of the most significant capabilities of today's electronic commerce environment, which was not possible earlier with respect to payoff examination, is the collection and analyses of tremendous volumes and types of data. Along with this capability comes the hope that we might be able to better utilize this data to make improved business decisions. An example is the analyses of click-stream data that helps in designing better Web sites or the analyses of customer profiles that can help in targeted marketing. However, data is only the first step. To paraphrase T.S. Eliot—Quite often information is lost in the data, knowledge is lost in the information and wisdom is lost in the knowledge.[1] Thus, the sequence from data to information to knowledge to wisdom needs to be complete to help in better decision making.

The capabilities of the e-commerce environment have facilitated data mining by combining mathematical and artificial intelligence algorithms with the rich data collection. Spurred by advances in information technology and data collection methods, data mining capitalizes on the availability of large data sets in commercial enterprises. This offers an unprecedented opportunity to analyze this data and extract useful information. The field of data mining draws upon extensive work in areas such as statistics, machine learning, pattern recognition, databases, and high-performance computing to discover interesting and previously unknown information in data sets.

An interesting example of benefits derived from data mining is the case of a major New York bank. The bank had a dial-up application that enabled customers to access their banking services. The application had few users and was targeted for discontinuation because of its high maintenance cost. What few users it had were constantly calling support to complain about the application. When a little data mining was done, it revealed that the very customers who used the application also happened to use other services of the bank and had a lot of

---

1. *Selected Poems*. T.S. Eliot, Harcourt Publishing, 1988.

money invested there. Most were elderly folk who used the customer support line as a social outlet. They called in and chatted with the support staff, whom they had come to know by name, using inadequacies of the software as an excuse to call in and chat. The application seemed to keep them connected with the bank and happy about doing their business there. Upon reflection, and the discerning of nonintuitively obvious relationships between the program, the customers, and other services that they used, decision makers at the bank decided to retain the application. Its dollar costs were more than offset by the value of the customer retention that it fostered. Thus, data mining is one of those areas that does not justify itself immediately in terms of return on investment, though it can provide enormous value to business decision making.

While data mining is at the front-end and a technology to extract information from data, customer relationship management (CRM) is involved with making business decisions with this information. For example, a catalog retailer has a new catalog and needs to determine which customers to target so there is a high likelihood that they will respond. The CRM process has a historical database of customers who responded to earlier catalogs and their profile. The CRM module would apply some built-in criteria to build a model of customer behavior that would then be used to predict which customers would be most likely to respond to the new catalog. This information can be used effectively to design targeted marketing strategies. Thus, payoffs can be more effectively realized in today's e-commerce environments, aided by data-mining and CRM modules. Such complementary changes can affect the extent of payoff and will require specialized approaches to capture.

E-commerce has also brought to the forefront the issue of payoff as a consequence of consumer loyalty. Does the e-commerce channel amplify or erode consumer loyalty? Does the medium have anything at all to do with consumer loyalty? We discuss these issues in the following section.

E-Loyalty: Your Payoff in Online Commerce

*"If you build a good site, users will come,
but if they visit only once, you lose."*

—Nielsen[2]

In business-to-consumer (B2C) e-commerce, does a traditional virtue like loyalty still stand on the high pedestal in the online world? After all, customers can defect with the click of a mouse. The unique economics of e-business make loyalty more important than ever. What are the metrics for loyalty? We believe that loyalty in cyberspace assumes even greater significance than loyalty in the physical marketplace. This is because it is very expensive to attract and obtain customers on the Internet, and unless these customers remain loyal and make repeat purchases, it is not a profitable proposition for the business. For example, it takes up to three years of customer loyalty for a credit card company to recover customer acquisition costs. In the payoff equation, therefore, loyalty in the online marketplace assumes a greater role than in traditional marketplaces.

In our analyses of data on online shoppers, we found surprisingly that loyalty to online shopping was significantly higher than conventional shopping. This runs counter to the common belief that customers are not as loyal to the online shopping channel as compared to physical or conventional stores. However, creating consumer loyalty is more complex than simply investing in electronic commerce initiatives. It requires a deeper understanding of what leads to consumer loyalty, and, therefore, how to capture it in the IT payoff equation.

---

2. Jakob Nielsen's Alertbox, August 1, 1997, *www.useit.com/alertbox/9708a.html.*

A MODEL FOR E-LOYALTY

Information technology in general has impacted businesses on any of the following metrics: productivity, profitability, and consumer surplus. In the case of electronic B2C commerce, the value to the customer may be derived from time savings, price, preferences, and ease of transaction. We suggest that the nature of the interaction between the customer and the Web presence of an online store also has an important effect on the purchase decision. Thus, features of the Web site that make the shopping experience for the customer a compelling experience contribute to the likelihood of a purchase decision. Satisfaction with purchases, experienced repeatedly, eventually leads to customer loyalty. We present a model and metrics for explaining customer loyalty in online shopping in Figure 10.1. Three factors contribute to satisfaction with the purchase: (1) the efficiency of the transaction as measured by metrics for ease of use, the effort required to search for the best product and complete the purchase, and

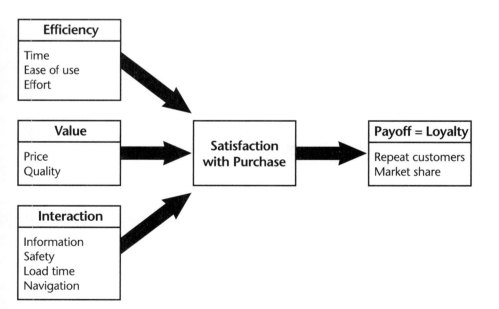

FIGURE 10.1 Model and metrics for online purchase.

the time involved in making a purchase; (2) the value to the customer realized either as a better price or better quality, or both, of the product or service; and (3) the nature of the interaction that might largely be a function of the design of the Web site. E-commerce represents an opportunity for enhancing customer satisfaction through each of these factors.

Customer loyalty is eventually what defines a sustained competitive advantage. The metrics for loyalty are increased market share, retention of customers, repeat purchases, and sales from retained customers versus new customers. Another question related to these metrics that we should ask ourselves is "Who are our most loyal customers?" Are they also our most profitable ones? For example, in the credit card and banking industries the most loyal customers might not be the profitable ones from the firm's perspective. Such an analysis might suggest appropriate customer segments to target to maximize payoff.

E-COMMERCE PAYOFF

In general, any technology can be viewed as yielding a payoff if it provides value. Value, in the electronic marketplace, can have varied connotations and oftentimes in ways that are very different from conventional marketplaces. Riggins developed on earlier work in communications technology to present an Electronic Commerce Value Grid to identify opportunities from e-commerce that provide value.[3] The first basic premise of this grid is that firms compete on five dimensions of commerce. They use various modes of *interaction* to compete over both *time* and *distance* with the objective of providing some *product* or *service* through a *chain of relationships*. Thus, the five dimensions are time, distance or geography, relationships, interactions, and product or service.

---

3. Frederick J. Riggins, "A Framework for Identifying Web-based Electronic Commerce Opportunities," *Journal of Organizational Computing and Electronic Commerce, 9* (1999): 297–310.

The second basic premise is that firms compete on these five dimensions to provide value along three payoff criteria: efficiency, effectiveness, and strategic advantage. Each of the 15 combinations represented by the 5×3 grid presents opportunities for providing value to the customer and thereby payoff from the technology. We build upon the dimensions of the electronic commerce value grid to present the payoff measures that would be the focus of IT payoff in these situations in Figure 10.2.

	PAYOFF		
	EFFICIENCY	EFFECTIVENESS	INNOVATION/ STRATEGIC
TIME	• *More tasks* • *Less error*	• *Number of clicks to access information*	• *Less load with a 24 × 7 service* • *Enhanced customer satisfaction*
GEOGRAPHY	• *Access to wider markets*	• *Search costs reduced with a single gateway access*	• *International sales* • *International customers*
RELATIONSHIPS	• *Time savings through use of intermediaries* • *Cost saving*	• *Customer response to micro-marketing*	• *Customer retention by creating dependency to lock-in users*
INTERACTION	• *Product improvements resulting from user feedback*	• *Click stream* • *Time*	• *COIN users*
PRODUCT/ SERVICE	• *Through use of agents* • *Better price* • *Less time*	• *Enhanced customer satisfaction through online decision support tools*	• *New products, services*

FIGURE 10.2 Payoff measures for electronic commerce.

How do today's businesses compete on the five dimensions mentioned in Figure 10.2? First, time has taken on tremendous significance in the business environment as businesses compete in Internet time. Everything from product design to development, testing, and marketing is done at amazingly high speeds compared to business a few years ago. Therefore, if a technology allows a company to achieve its tasks faster, the technology is perceived as having a payoff. In the electronic marketplace, distance and geography have far less significance. Another key aspect that has changed since the advent of electronic commerce is the nature of the relationship between customers and businesses. By offering new functionalities (such as 24 × 7 access to account information), smaller and newer businesses can challenge established, bigger competitors. E-commerce might also add value to customers through relationships that are established through online communities (COINS, communities of interest). Finally, e-commerce presents opportunities to offer new products or to bundle existing products and services that were not possible through traditional modes of business. Thus, all five dimensions present avenues for realizing value from the technology and thereby enhancing payoff from it.

While the dimensions discussed above offer opportunities for realizing value from e-commerce technologies, what exactly is the mechanism for creating value? It is through the channels of increased effectiveness, efficiency, and strategic advantage or innovation. Effectiveness is doing the right thing, while efficiency is doing the thing right. So, efficiency comes with doing certain tasks such as bill payment or procurement more efficiently using Web-based technologies. Effectiveness, on the other hand, is associated with improved decision making because of the timely information made available by e-commerce, such as finding the right flight depending upon limitations of time, cost, and number of connections. Finally, electronic commerce can result in strategic advantage if the technology allows the business to enter new markets or offer new bundles of products and services that can garner greater market share. An example would be Federal Express' feature for customers to check the status of their package at any time.

Each intersection of the dimensions of commerce and dimensions of value creation can be viewed as a potential for payoff from the electronic commerce-based business.

On the dimension of time, e-commerce adds value to the customer, and thereby payoff from the technology, by enabling the customer to accomplish a wide array of tasks in relatively quick time. For example, Land's End allows a customer to view a catalog, see how a particular dress would look, order online, and get an estimate of when the product would be delivered. Another example is using online banking to transfer funds, pay bills, check balances, and so on. These represent a more efficient way of conducting business than traditional modes and therefore, from the customer's perspective, add value. Payoff metrics that can be used in this case are the number of tasks possible, the number of errors, and so on.

Today's age can be characterized as the Information Age. Yet, the constant bombardment of a barrage of information makes businesses and individuals yearn for useful knowledge. To make effective decisions, one has to gather knowledge by wading through a lot of information. E-commerce can make this process more effective by providing only the desired information. An example is CNN Interactive, which provides news updates on areas that the customer has expressed interest. A metric can be developed to assess the payoff on this dimension that incorporates the time and number of screens, on the average, before the user accesses the information sought.

A strategic benefit from e-commerce technologies, for example, for banks and the IRS, is that they not only can provide the right information but can also do this 7 days a week, 24 hours a day. Direct benefits accrued might be captured as metrics for less load at the bank, and higher customer satisfaction.

Along the dimension of "distance," e-commerce can allow even small players to get access to larger markets. By setting up a Web presence and a storefront, even small businesses that originally were restricted to local markets now have the capability to present themselves in the national marketplace. E-commerce allows several smaller entities to come together so that they can overcome scale and combat bigger players. An example is autobytel.com, which brings together thousands of smaller automobile dealers so that they are able to compete with the large dealerships.[4] The number of markets and customers e-commerce technology provides access to might serve as metrics to examine this dimension.

E-commerce technologies can make information access more effective for customers by providing a single gateway of access and then directing or filtering users to relevant sites. Many companies now have a single point of access that provides all the information about a company, including products, prices, availability, and contacts within the company. Thus, search costs for the customer are substantially reduced compared to the time when customers had to get on the phone to get basic account information. Measures for the time and effort involved in searching and accessing information would serve as metrics to assess payoff.

The biggest strategic advantage of electronic commerce to many small businesses is the promise of global visibility and access to global markets. Companies such as 1-800-FLOWERS are niche players that now have a global presence, thanks to the Internet.[5] Customers and sales from global markets are a reflection of payoff along this dimension.

The side of electronic commerce that many did not foresee was its ability to alter the nature of the relationship between the customer and the business. One way in which the Internet has changed this relationship is through intermediaries. Customers can make decisions more efficiently because of businesses that specialize in collecting, analyzing, and compiling information about the various options available and thus make the decision-making process for the customer more efficient. These types of businesses are termed "intermediaries" or "infomediaries." The other way in which the relationship has changed is through the opposite mechanism—that of disinter-

---

4. Frederick J. Riggins, "A Framework for Identifying Web-based Electronic Commerce Opportunities," *Journal of Organizational Computing and Electronic Commerce,* 9 (1999): 297–310.

5. Ibid.

mediation. That is, companies, especially computer manufacturers, are doing away with retailers and distributors and selling direct to the customer. Both intermediation and disintermediation offer value and payoff under various circumstances. The bottom line is the benefits to customers measured along metrics of cost and time savings. It provides another channel to many organizations looking to broaden their presence, and to cut down on the cost of typical intermediaries, such as brokers.

Market research often groups customers based on their similarities into several clusters. The objective of such an exercise is that we can learn more about these groups and tailor our marketing efforts based on these profiles. Taking this argument to its logical limit is the possibility of every customer being a market. This is exactly what today's e-commerce technologies can provide by keeping track of the shopping and surfing habits of individual customers. Therefore, companies, such as Amazon.com, can then tailor their marketing efforts to every individual customer. This is referred to as one-to-one (1:1) marketing. This way, even large businesses can appear to look micro by providing individualized attention to customers. "Customer response rates to targeted marketing" is a useful metric that can be compared to traditional response rates to examine the payoff in this context.

A strategic approach through which companies create a lock-in of customers into longer-term relationships is by providing some services free of charge and charge for other advanced services. An example might be an investment firm that attracts customers to its site by providing real-time quotes. However, more detailed financial analyses and stock recommendation might be available to only customers of that bank. In this context, it is the technology that is providing the capability to do so and thereby is a payoff from the technology.

E-commerce technologies have also altered the nature of the interaction between the customer and the business. This aspect can be exploited by businesses to understand the customer better. For example, McGraw-Hill has a Beta Book site where users can view completed books and provide their feedback online.[6] These are then incorporated into the final version of the book that is sent for print. In this example, the payoff from the technology is that it provides the capability to improve the product substantially before the product is actually launched into the market. Metrics for product improvement and time-to-market, which are context-dependent, might serve as payoff metrics.

Effectiveness, from the standpoint of the user's information-gathering capabilities, is vastly improved using e-commerce technologies. Online catalogs and news providers design their Web sites in such a way that the user can quickly drill down to an area of interest and then obtain greater detail. Many companies follow the "three-click" rule, such that any information that a customer desires can be accessed within three mouse clicks. Such designs provide value to customers of a business and should also be factored into the payoff equation. Realizing that companies are recognizing the value from metrics that are developed from click-stream data, many companies now specialize in collecting and analyzing such data.

Finally, the new forms of interaction provided by e-commerce can be tapped for strategic advantage through the formation of "community of interest" (COIN) groups. Examples are discussion groups on Netscape or ESPN. The interaction between different users with similar interests as a result of the business' Web site creates a lock-in and increased loyalty to the business. Thus, such online communities can serve to create loyal customers in the long run. Again, such payoffs are very unique to e-commerce technologies. Metrics that can inform the situation are the number of users, the traffic, and the loyalty of users of COIN groups.

Electronic commerce has been viewed as a "disruptive technology" because it has the potential to change the dynamics of the existing market by creating new products and services that might cannibalize the old. One way they can

---

6.   Frederick J. Riggins, "A Framework for Identifying Web-based Electronic Commerce Opportunities," *Journal of Organizational Computing and Electronic Commerce, 9* (1999): 297–310.

achieve this is through providing greater efficiency for online shoppers through agent technology. These are automated agents that search the Web for the best price for a particular product. With the development of such technologies customers have at their fingertips the ability to identify the best prices and availability of products within seconds. Again, we need to explicitly recognize the ability of today's e-commerce technologies to achieve this as a payoff as well. Price savings, time spent, and product information gained via such technologies are all metrics of payoff.

How do e-commerce technologies provide new products/services that help customers make more effective decisions? Examples are Schwab's IRA Analyzer and Turner Broadcasting's Turner Mania.[7] Schwab's IRA Analyzer which helps individual investors determine the optimal IRA for their situation. In other words, the Internet can present a decision support tool for users. Turner Broadcasting's Turner Mania which allows advertising executives to develop targeted advertising campaigns. A direct payoff from incorporating such features to provide decision support will be increased customer satisfaction and loyalty.

Finally, new products and services can be created through e-commerce by bundling various products or services or by using new capabilities of the technology. For example, many real estate companies have streaming videos of the homes they sell where potential buyers can view the inside and outside of the home and also have a virtual tour of the home. The same technology is also revolutionizing the way news is delivered, of course subject to bandwidth restrictions. An example of a Web site gaining a strategic advantage by bringing together previously disparate categories is Amazon.com. It is able to attract a large membership because it has various offerings at the same site.

---

7. Frederick J. Riggins, "A Framework for Identifying Web-based Electronic Commerce Opportunities," *Journal of Organizational Computing and Electronic Commerce,* 9 (1999): 297–310.

In summary, Web technologies offer a real opportunity to push the envelope and offer new products and services that might have significant gains in efficiency and effectiveness, and provide a strategic advantage. Some of these are easier to measure than others, but the bottom line is that there should be an explicit recognition of these benefits as a payoff from the technology.

The above discussion presents the capabilities of e-commerce and how many organizations are utilizing these capabilities to create customer value. However, the promise of e-commerce has yet to be fully realized. Several challenges remain on the path to exploiting the potential of payoff from e-commerce.

LOOKING TO THE FUTURE: CHALLENGES IN IT PAYOFF ASSESSMENT

Digital dotcoms versus physical dotcoms. Digital dotcoms are Internet-based companies whose products or services are digital in nature and therefore delivered over the Internet, while physical dotcoms are companies whose products are physical but yet the company has a Web-front for customers to buy products. How does IT payoff vary for digital dotcoms versus physical dotcoms? Initial evidence[8] suggests that IT capital (computer software, hardware, and networking equipment) contributed significantly to revenues and margins for digital dotcoms but not for physical dotcoms. Thus, the physical dotcoms need to work extra hard to translate IT investment into business results.

New metrics. The e-commerce era has brought a plethora of new metrics. Some of these are a function of the conscious technology investment decisions by the company as well as the customer interaction with the company. Examples include bandwidth, traffic, number of hits, number of unique visitors,

---

8. A. Barua, Y. Fang, and A.B. Whinston, "Not All Dot-coms Are Created Equal," Working paper, University of Texas at Austin, 1999.

connection time, and "stickiness" of Web sites. While the technology offers the opportunity to monitor these metrics, the challenge is relating these to business performance. Just because one invests in IT to increase the bandwidth need not necessarily mean better business performance for the company. This payoff equation can be computed using some of the techniques mentioned in this book.

Management of change. Technologically speaking, the last few years have witnessed more change than the decade preceding that, and this is likely to be true for the next decade as well. Thus, the challenge of implementing new technologies and managing this change has become an everyday reality in companies. Change management skills coupled with objective metrics will help in the realization of payoff in this changing environment. An example is Cisco systems switching from Windows 95 to Windows 2000. One of the metrics that was tracked was the number of blue screens, that is, a locked operating system. While this might appear to be an insignificant change, converting over 30,000 workstations worldwide can cause significant disruption in the operations. Furthermore, this change is one of several change initiatives within the company, and not to mention the changes at the market and economy level. The e-commerce age is likely to impose several such software and hardware upgrades to existing technologies. In order for companies to exact payoff from IT, they will have to develop effective mechanisms for managing technological change.

Balance of power. Electronic commerce has played the part of a disruptive technology on changing the balance of power in many business relationships. A classic example is reverse auctions. Say General Electric is interested in finding a publisher to print catalogs and brochures for its various products. GE now puts this on the Web and lets publishers bid for the contract. Rather than going out and looking for publishers, GE lets publishers bid for its job. The same situation is true for a homeowner who is interested in securing a mortgage. Reverse auctions allow various banks and financing agencies across the country to bid for the homeowner's mortgage. The shift of power in this relationship implies that the payoff will certainly be better for the party that gains power through e-commerce.

Cascading effects. The most promising projections in terms of the use of e-commerce are in the area of business-to-business (B2B) commerce. From a payoff perspective, use of B2B offers numerous direct benefits such as increased efficiency and speed. However, there might be several associated benefits such as improved forecasting of business requirements between business partners. The challenge in these B2B situations is to implement and evaluate metrics to measure forecast errors that might be reduced as a result of B2B commerce or work-in-process inventory that might be reduced due to more timely orders and supplies.

Value of collaboration. One of the paradoxes of electronic commerce is that one area that it has the biggest impact in is improving coordination, yet it is this coordination that has been the most difficult to evaluate. What were coordination costs before the advent of e-commerce and what are the coordination costs after adopting e-commerce? This is a difficult and challenging question and might be key to justifying the payoff from e-commerce. Several companies have reaped the benefits of this by placing the burden of tracking and maintaining their inventory on the vendor, called vendor-managed inventory (VMI). Some outcomes of better coordination are fewer forecast errors and reduced inventory costs. Sometimes, improvements in processes result merely from the fact that the buyer and the seller understand and are thinking about the process. An example is that during the flu season, an antihistamine manufacturer may collaborate with a retail pharmacy chain to come up with a suitable quantity of the medicine for its various outlets. By collaborating, the retailer optimizes the space, reduces drug expirations, and returns to the manufacturer. At the same time, the manufacturer is able to develop a suitable production and distribution plan while reducing the likelihood of stockouts or overproductions.

The area of collaboration will continue to offer the most opportunities, as well as challenges, in payoff estimation in the years to come. Managers and users of technology will have to think outside their mental straitjackets to devise new metrics to examine the payoff equation in these scenarios.

11

ASSESSING
IT PAYOFF:
A CASE STUDY

To illustrate the application of the EIAC model (Chapter 9), this chapter presents the experience of one healthcare company in coming to the realization that IT payoff needs to be measured and eventually setting up a system to continuously capture and analyze information technology payoff. Although the case study discusses data and issues from the healthcare industry, the case information is relevant in other industries. For example, we find that challenges such as collaborating with business managers to develop metrics, translating business requirements into technical imperatives, and demonstrating the value of IT to senior management, are virtually the same in all industries. Just the extent may vary.

As you read this case study, think about the issues facing your organization and how you would approach these steps. In the next chapter, we will present a summary of the discussion followed by concrete steps to help initiate and sustain an IT payoff project in an organization.

PHASE 1: EXPLORATION

First, a bit of company background followed by the competitive, organizational, and political climate. Then we show how one IT executive's vision led to a project in IT payoff leading to a buy-in and eventually establishment of an IT payoff mechanism.

The company, which we refer to as Ardent, is a multi-entity national organization with its headquarters in the midwest region of the United States. While the entities implement and maintain operational systems, the strategic financial and clinical information systems reside at the corporate office. The investment in these corporate systems is the subject of our case study. The strategic information system (SIS) supports functions such as contract evaluation, quality management, process redesign, cost allocation, profitability analysis, and clinical treatment effectiveness analysis. The SISs are supported by data from operational financial and billing systems, combined by customer satisfaction and clinical outcomes. Continuous investment in SIS has expanded existing functionality as well as added new data and there are proposals for further investment to add functionality and upgrade the technology platforms. Occasionally, the organization has been concerned about whether the benefits returned are worth the technology investment, not the least of which is whether or not they are using the technology effectively.

While reading an IT payoff article in a trade magazine, the SIS executive said to himself, "I don't think we have ever tried to see what the technology is contributing to the organization's bottom line." He recalled that a manager had once proposed conducting a study, and that proposal was never given attention because the organization had never felt the need to explore payoff issues. Why? The company had been operating at a 10%–12% profit margin, well above the industry average.

The executives didn't want to invest in spending time and effort when the bottom line demonstrated that we must have been doing something right! After all, the company's SIS had been cited in the press as one of the best in the industry. So, why bother?

At about the same time, another SIS professional noticed the debate in academic circles about whether IT does pay off? As the two SIS executives were working on the proposal, the CIO reported that requests from the user community would require upgrades to the functionality as well as the technology platform for SIS.

The CIO's office, with assistance from other executives, prepared a proposal for enhanced functionality in the SIS. The first phase of the investment would go for software development and consulting services. Because the technology was over a decade old, future sustained investment would be required for migrating the technology platform from mainframe computers to a Web-enabled client–server system with superior reporting capabilities.

STEP 1: IDENTIFYING THE INVESTMENT STAGE

We pick up this discussion from the boardroom scene in the opening of this book where the senior management asked the CIO if he can demonstrate that the past IT appropriations returned value to the organization. The underlying concerns of the senior management were: How can we be certain if the new investment will improve the efficiency and profitability of the company? And, if this is the case, are the benefits greater than the investment? Can we learn from the past investment as to what works and does not work so that we can target the investment to more profitable areas?

Most organizations can relate to the fact that as long as they do well financially, few questions get asked to justify investment. As competition heats up and the bottom line shrinks, there is greater pressure to justify the investment. This was the case of the health system. As reimbursement of services reduced, calls for demonstrated business value increased.

Although measuring IT payoff had not been mandated, SIS executives began researching the SIS payoff for the reimbursement modeling application. The modeling application was used by decision makers to model expected reimbursement from insurance companies for services rendered to insured patients. The modeling system is a crucial SIS because it assists managers in controlling costs and helps in contract negotiations with insurance companies. Above all, the value of the modeling system has been its ability to recommend or decline contracts, depending upon their financial potential.

STEP 2: MATCH APPROACH AND TECHNIQUES

Given that the reinvestment stage deals with enhancing the existing system, primarily through the upgrade technology, the functionality of the system will remain essentially the same. It is apparent from the above discussion that management is interested in assessing if the SIS has paid off in the past and continues to do so. Therefore, the approach to assessing IT payoff should be to assess the costs of running the system, the usage of the system, and how it has benefited the hospitals in improving quality of services and profitability. Any evidence of improved business processes resulting from the use of SIS will also be considered as an impact.

The techniques for exploring such relationships will involve establishing correlation between the variables of investment with variables of interest such as quality or profitability indicators, evaluating the regression equation to gauge the extent of investment variables' contribution in improving quality or profitability. However, to do so we need to identify what the metrics or variables are that we should capture for the next two phases.

PHASE II: INVOLVEMENT

STEP 3: IDENTIFY TANGIBLE AND INTANGIBLE METRICS

Ardent categorized the types of metrics into three groups for ease of identification and analysis: performance metrics, IT metrics, and control metrics. Performance metrics relate to the performance of the organization or department. This is typically the impetus for the IT expenditure—to increase revenue, improve satisfaction, and so on. The IT metrics are various ways to capture IT-related spending or investment. And the control metrics are factors that also affect performance, but which are not IT-related. However, it is important to account for, or control for, their effects in the analysis.

Along the above categorization, Ardent identified various relevant metrics. For performance, the net patient revenue per admission was an important indicator of financial performance. As measures of quality of service are provided, data about patient satisfaction were tracked. IT-related investments were monitored along the traditional accounting categories of labor, support, and capital. Finally, control variables or context variables were the amount of Medicare, Medicaid services provided, patient income, and hospital age.

STEPS 4 AND 5: MAKE BUSINESS CASE FOR IT PAYOFF MEASUREMENT AND ENSURE CUSTOMER INVOLVEMENT

In making the business case, Ardent ensured that the various entities that would provide data were informed of the intent of the study. Among many constituents, such as quality and finance departments, the attempt to measure the impact of IT was welcomed perhaps because they are accustomed to measuring quantitative outcomes. However, some areas appeared resistant to spending time and effort that, in their view, would not affect productivity. Some appeared skeptical of the stated intent that the analysis might be a precursor to layoffs or outsourcing.

To counter such perception, the initial communication indicated that the analysis would focus on SIS spending and how decision makers used the SIS, not people or their positions. The follow-up discussions with managers also stated that the organization is adopting a continuous improvement approach (a term that everyone in manufacturing and healthcare understands) to evaluate past investments so that future investments are strategically made. As people used the SIS across the organization, making the connection to business functions was not required. If the SIS were a financial system, the linkage with other functions and the importance of such an evaluation would have been necessary.

Nevertheless, this step was not easy. Managers found their own ways to make the business case for the study. It did not help that the company was financially better off than its competitors, because that created a sense of "why bother" among the users. On the other hand, the case for measurement was helped by the fact that the industry as a whole was not particularly strong. By pointing to some of the failures in the industry, managers were able to make their case so that most people involved understood the intent of the study and were willing to provide the data.

PHASE III: ANALYSIS

STEP 6: CONDUCT ANALYSIS

Labor, capital, and support represented the SIS investment; while the organization level payoff was captured by revenue per admission and revenue per day, as well as expenses and rate of reimbursement from insurance companies for treating their patients.

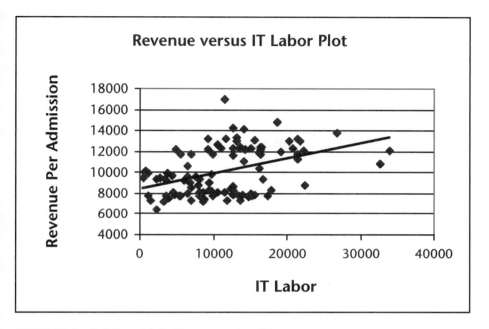

FIGURE 11.1 Preliminary analysis of investment and payoff data.

The first step in the analysis is to examine if there is a relationship between hospital performance and IT investment using simple graphs. As an example, we show the plot between revenue and IT labor in Figure 11.1. The data were disguised to protect the confidentiality of competitively sensitive information. From the figure, it should be apparent that as the investment in IT labor increases the revenue per admission also increases. In other words, there is a direct linear relationship between these two variables.

Given the linear relationship between hospital financial performance and investment in IT labor, we proceed to use the techniques described in earlier chapters by examining models for each performance measure. The technique employed is regression analysis, which is available in Microsoft Excel. This can be accessed by going to the Tools pull-down menu option and selecting Data Analysis, and then selecting Regression from the pull-down menu (see also Chapter 8). (Note: If you do not see Data Analysis, choose Add-in from the Tools menu, then check on Analysis ToolPak in the dialog box and then try the above steps.)

The next stage is to specify the various metrics that have to be incorporated in the analysis. In regression terminology, the hospital performance will be the Y range and all the variables that relate to IT investments as well as the control variables will be the X range. The data corresponding to these metrics have to be highlighted as input to the regression analysis. The following output (Figure 11.2) is obtained for the model with the net patient revenue per admission as the performance metric.

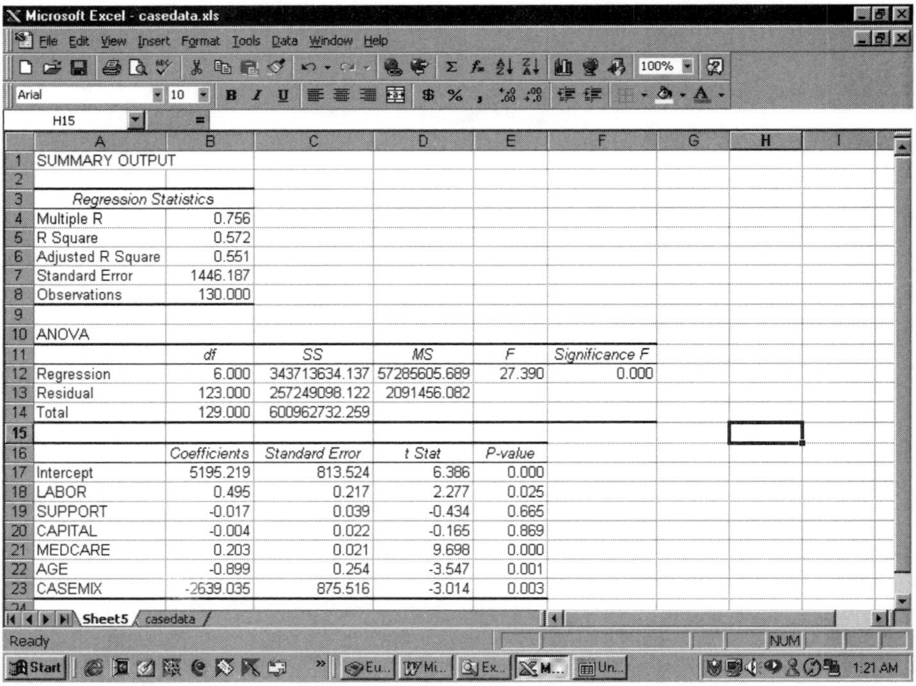

SUMMARY OUTPUT					
Regression Statistics					
Multiple R	0.756				
R Square	0.572				
Adjusted R Square	0.551				
Standard Error	1446.187				
Observations	130.000				
ANOVA					
	df	*SS*	*MS*	*F*	*Significance F*
Regression	6.000	343713634.137	57285605.689	27.390	0.000
Residual	123.000	257249098.122	2091456.082		
Total	129.000	600962732.259			
	Coefficients	*Standard Error*	*t Stat*	*P-value*	
Intercept	5195.219	813.524	6.386	0.000	
LABOR	0.495	0.217	2.277	0.025	
SUPPORT	-0.017	0.039	-0.434	0.665	
CAPITAL	-0.004	0.022	-0.165	0.869	
MEDCARE	0.203	0.021	9.698	0.000	
AGE	-0.899	0.254	-3.547	0.001	
CASEMIX	-2639.035	875.516	-3.014	0.003	

FIGURE 11.2 Regression analysis using investment variables.

STEP 7: INTERPRET DATA FOR CONSTITUENTS

An inference about the impact of IT investment on hospital revenue is based on the values in the columns labeled Coefficients and P-value. The coefficients indicate by how much performance increases when the input variable (say labor) increases by one unit. The P-value indicates the probability of finding a relationship this strong between the input and performance variables by random chance. Thus, P-values less than 0.01 (10%) can be considered as indicative of a significant relationship.

As can be seen, the labor component of the IT investment alone has a significant impact on hospital revenue. Among the non-IT variables, Medicare, age, and case mix are significantly associated with revenue. The finding for IT labor suggests that when an investment in IT labor is increased by one unit, the hospital revenue increases by 0.495 units after accounting for all the other variables. The finding that IT support and capital did not have a significant impact on hospital revenue is worth noting. This is perhaps because IT support and capital are one-time investments and continued profitability requires continued labor. The analysis (not reported here) further indicated that when the IT investment is combined with process reengineering, the impact on profitability is more pronounced. Furthermore, the study also found a lag effect of three periods. Since our data collection is by month, this implies that the impact of IT investment appears in about three months.

The number labeled R-square is 0.572, and indicates that the model explains 57.2% of the variation in hospital revenue. In other words, while other factors such as the sickness level of patients and the type of patients can make a difference in profitability, IT investment determines a good part of it.

PHASE IV: COMMUNICATION

STEP 8: PROVIDE FEEDBACK AND ACTIONABLE STEPS

Nothing upsets functional department managers more than a thick binder with a copy of a report without an explanation about what it means and what needs to be done. We found several past studies laying on the office shelves gathering dust. Managers told us of their wasted time and effort in helping consultants write the report. The reports repeated what they already knew, while other parts were not explained.

In the case of Ardent, the feedback was provided in several forms. First, the people who helped directly in providing data were provided the results in person. The implications of the results and the meaning for their department were articulated. For instance, the organizations that reported higher activity of process redesign in clinical areas demonstrated lower costs and higher revenues. Actionable steps, indicating how redesign of clinical pathways when combined with better information systems to track services, were likely to improve productivity.

Other forms of feedback, such as short descriptions of projects, their outcomes, and the savings to organizations, were provided through the corporate Web site for the consumption of general employees so that future projects can be identified. The Web site also provided contact names for past projects as well as people responsible if one wanted to start a new project. In addition, analysts within IT and finance departments attended meetings of user groups representing several functional areas. For instance, a presentation was made at the accounting managers' meeting to demonstrate how the SIS could be used in identifying a higher percentage of variable costs. In addition, an illustration of the impact of standardizing the general ledger on the corporation's ability to identify areas of process redesign and improvement was provided.

STEP 9: INSTITUTIONALIZE BIAS FOR IT PAYOFF MEASUREMENT

As the results of the payoff analysis were shared across organizations, the purpose of why the analysis was conducted and the vision of the payoff analysis were also expressed. It was the buy-in of the process that was of equal interest to senior management. Discussion of its importance took place at all levels ranging from the senior management council to departmental meetings initiating several new projects.

Institutionalization of the bias for measurement was prompted by the reward and recognition mechanism advanced by the management at Ardent. Individuals who attempted payoff of their investment were recognized through the Web site and at corporate events. Furthermore, their visibility in the organization also increased when they were invited by other departments to speak about the initiation and execution of the payoff analysis. The organization also made an effort to reward such employees through performance bonuses and promotions. Department managers were shown how the payoff analysis encompassed improvement in productivity, quality of outcomes, and customer service, in addition to profitability. This is important because not all departments are revenue-producing departments, yet expenditures in IT are made across the board.

Once the payoff analysis was accepted by the users, several IT systems instituted metrics for automatic capture of revenue, expenses, investments, and other variables needed to calculate payoff. The institutional bias was clearly proven when the payoff metric was made a part of the senior management's "dashboard" indicators. Dashboard indicators are also a part of the report card to the board of directors.

AN UPDATE

Resulting from the success of the payoff measurement projects, Ardent has initiated several new initiatives in measuring the value of strategic purchasing systems, contract evaluation, and impact of information systems to track medication errors. This is in addition to examining the payoff of previous systems in light of training, and the intensity of process reengineering. Early reports indicate better cooperation among departments and formation of cross-entity teams to share best practices supported by data from the SIS.

CONCLUSION

This chapter has reported a part of the payoff analysis in one organization. The case is presented through the lens of the EIAC framework. We are certain that there were other factors, such as interpersonal relationships, loyalty to the company, and the interest of key individuals, that played a role in the success of the payoff project. You will have to give some thought to the means, including people and politics, to implement successful projects in your organization. You may also find that some education is necessary to gain support of key individuals in the organization.

Having read the example of Ardent, you may be wondering: How does this case help me? What can I do within my organization to implement an IT payoff project? Where should I begin? Chapter 12 summarizes the material discussed thus far as well as provides actionable steps relating to the EIAC model (as discussed in Chapter 9).

INTERVIEW WITH JIM ELERT, CIO, TRINITY HEALTH

How do you go about measuring IT payoff in healthcare?

Jim Elert (JE): In healthcare we have a good idea of what it costs but we have a difficult time figuring out the ROI. A simple way to look at payoff is to measure value, where value = benefit/costs. The issue is that value is perceived value resulting from the benefit we are providing. The numerator has not been clear.

INTERVIEW WITH JIM ELERT, CIO, TRINITY HEALTH

How do you measure payoff when the benefits are unclear?

JE: We have entered into internal service level agreements where we ask our constituents, "What is important to you in the service we provide?" We have a conversation with them about their perception of benefits and value. For example, "I can give this application to you in four days but have to hire two more people." How much is it worth to you? Would you pay for it?

How do you allocate these costs? Do the costs go to the department that got the service?

JE: We submit a budget to the corporate office, that is, we know the denominator. The question is, "Who will pay what percentage of the cost?" There is then an allocation model with an algorithm that computes the cost allocation based upon our discussions. In the past, it was a historical percentage that each SBU [strategic business unit] paid and it did not take into account what services they used. We got the CFOs to agree on how to relate the services they receive, for example, the number of applications, phone lines, etc., that they use. Then we turned up the crank. Based on that we figured how much of the systems their people were using. We found that there were winners and there were losers. Some had been underpaying for years and some were paying more than their share. But the CFOs had already agreed on the algorithm.

How did you choose the measures for your algorithms?

JE: We picked measures that are easier to measure. We don't go into the minutiae such as how much disk space you use and how many minutes we spent on answering a service call. At some point the cost of capturing the data exceeds the benefit from it.

Are there additional expectations on how IT has to be measured?

JE: In the clinical arena, there is an expectation that quality has to be measured in assessing IT payoff. In assessing how well the hospitals meet their objectives, the senior management team now uses clinical quality as opposed to just financial outcomes.

How is the quality measurement proceeding?

JE: They are beginning to come up with quality indicators. The measurements are being reported and pressure is being felt.

How do you link quality and clinical investment?

JE: Let me illustrate this with an example. We are installing an Adverse Drug Event (ADE) system. This is a system that monitors the drugs being administered to patients and matches them with other drugs, their laboratory tests, and other diagnostic data to ensure that there is no adverse effect. This used to be a manual process the pharmacists go through. The ADE system alerts the care provider or pharmacist when there is such a likelihood of an event, so it is like a quality indicator.

As a measure of the payoff of IT investment, we are measuring the number of times the alerts are fired. Then we count the number of times the physician changes the drug order, based on the ADE system's alerts. Now, many times the alerts fire and people already knew of that event. But the real payoff comes at those times it could be a problem and care is changed. We are now measuring the ADE before and after the system was implemented. Therefore, the financial payoff has to be tied to the quality event, one that the users perceive as value to them.

Have you quantified the value of one ADE or one more satisfied customer?

JE: Only in isolated cases. It is a negotiation with the recipient of the service. How much cost are people willing to bear. They want to know how much can you give me for this cost. For them, this is maximizing value.

In your annual report, how do you show value for each hospital whose perception of value may differ?

JE: Definitely by each hospital. We go to each CEO and present them the statistics for the year. We share with them the services we provide, such as applications, the ratio of support people to devices, etc.

Selling the IT services, even internally, is a key part of creating value because there is corporate perception of value and then there is a hospital perception of value. Corporations would like to see common quality indicators, common databases, and same systems across the organization to oversee organizational performance while benefiting from lower costs resulting from economies of scale.

In regard to strategic versus operation value, how do you differentiate between the two in selling the idea to hospitals?

JE: We had an IS summit meeting of the hospital senior leadership in which we discussed that every IS investment has an ROI. We learned from them that there are other reasons, besides financial ROI, such as those compliance issues where the systems are mandated by the market or government. The conclusion of the meeting was that in such cases it was not necessary to have financial impact analysis. The question then becomes, "How much cost has to absorbed, putting aside the issue whether or not there are financial benefits?" In many cases, we don't know that yet so we rely on projections or others' experiences. For example, there is extensive literature that each time there is an ADE, there is a cost of $5,000. This is not counting the cost in human suffering and litigation, etc. Therefore, for such systems, we can use this number to justify the IT payoff.

However, there is a precursor to this. You cannot do effective and ongoing payoff analysis without standardization as a foundation. A few years ago in our corporation, every PC was configured differently. You cannot put together meaningful metrics when each PC is a "work of art" and it takes three weeks to set up a PC. Once a PC is standardized, then you can begin to talk meaningfully about how long it takes to fix a PC problem.

What did you do to ensure standardization?

JE: We standardized at several levels. First, we standardized the desktops of each user. The next major standardization was consolidating the data centers. Each hospital's data center used to have different ways of doing things, for example, disaster recovery standards. Now that there is one data center, we can tell you how much time it takes to recover from a failure, what our process is to announce downtime to the users because there are now standard procedures. Finally, we are ensuring the standardization of applications. We believe in the "design once, implement many times" for a common core set of applications. It will allow us to track usage, performance, and outcomes.

Is there a difference in standardization of hardware versus software?

JE: For hardware it is centralizing. For applications software it is the processes being implemented. For instance, to implement order entry systems a standardized workflow will be easier to measure across the organization.

How do you get buy-in from people whose work processes are going to change as a result of the new systems being put in?

JE: There are many different views. Some have indicated that we should just "slam in" the new application because they don't want to spend time and money in redesigning work processes. At the other end of the spectrum are people who expect us to invest in automating the optimum solutions.

How do you develop these metrics?

JE: Our customer services group involved potentially affected parties in coming up with the measurements and what they basically did *they had some users.* IS didn't come up with what we're going to measure.

What are your thoughts on technology and the competitive advantage in healthcare?

JE: I think that quality is going to win the day. That's measuring and ensuring a high clinical quality of care. I think we're going to look at it that way as a competitive advantage. Things that are going to improve quality, I think eventually they are going to start to really feature in our activities. It's just not an area you can afford to fall behind in.

If you have your way, what would be your ideal way of measuring the impact in being able to show value to a corporation?

JE: There's no simple answer to that question. There are ways that IS will have to demonstrate value to an organization. The issue is that the product here is the health of a person. It's not something that you can stamp out on an assembly line. It's incredibly complex. Human beings are complex. And so all these disciplines have grown up. The clinical world is a world unto itself. So are the pathology labs and pharmacies. They have cultures. Think miniature cultures and they're different for the hospital. IT has to serve these complex clienteles and the products they deliver are multifaceted. The metrics will need to be developed collaboratively and represent the multifaceted nature of the business.

Jim Elert earned a BS in Computer Science from Michigan State University in 1976 and has been in the healthcare computing field ever since. He has served in a variety of provider organizations and is currently CIO for Trinity Health, the seventh largest healthcare provider organization in the United States.

12 SUCCEEDING AT IT PAYOFF MEASUREMENT: AN ACTION PLAN

*"Computers are useless.
They can only give you answers."*

—PABLO PICASSO

W̲e conclude our discussion of information technology payoff with a summary of key ideas proposed in the book, followed by an action plan on how to implement an IT payoff measurement initiative in your organization.

The challenge of managing and evaluating information technology has become more complicated as the investment has continued to grow. The IT function will have to stand on its own and demonstrate business and strategic value. While it is easier to calculate payoff for operational information technology, it is far more challenging and critical to measure and show value of strategic IT investments. That is why it is easier to measure outsourcing IT applications, which generally involve identifiable and tangible IT. That is also why it is extremely difficult to measure the true payoff of investing in a collaborative planning, forecasting, and replenishment system to go with ERP. This is, however, not a good reason not to attempt measurement. The strategy document should be a guide to the objectives of the investment. Look for the impetus that led to the decision to IT investment in the first place. If you are yet to invest, find out what the "yardstick" is by which the investment will be judged a success, both formal and informal. Look for where the organization's "pain" is and who is feeling it the most. You might find this in the minutes of the strategy meetings. Also look for the "squeaky wheels"—the constituents that have the ear of senior management. Often these are people or departments that set the tone, good or bad, for the perception of IT payoff.

RECAP

Through Porter's two models (see Chapter 2), look for areas of opportunity in the business landscape. Study where the organization is best positioned to take advantage of its strengths—its people, existing infrastructure, reputation, and market share. Technology should measure its value parallel to the business value. That means that if the business assesses its success by the number of new customers acquired, then IT should also measure its success by demonstrating how it enabled the business in finding, signing up, and retaining new customers. Similarly, if the core competency is the lowest failure of a manufactured part in the industry, then IT should show its support in designing, testing, tracking, and communicating the causes of failure.

It is likely that in spite of aligning the investment with strategy and establishing proper metrics, the payoff will remain elusive (see Chapter 3). Don't get distracted by the talk of productivity paradox. Recent studies have largely dismissed it. Besides, the IT productivity paradox discussion applies to macro-evaluation of IT payoff, generally at the industry and economy levels. Each industry consists of organizations that range from well managed to mediocre and also those that squander the IT investment. This is not to imply that IT investment will always show payoff. Sometimes, despite the best strategy and measurement tools, the payoff will not show up.

Competition's counterstrategy, changing consumer preferences, substituting products and services, and bad timing can be some reasons. Assess if the impetus of investment is to keep the customers. When MCI implemented its Friends and Family long-distance telephone calling plan, its competitor, AT&T, had to respond by a similar plan. AT&T invested in modifying its billing systems and offered its own customer retention plan. In this case, the IT would be considered strategic even if the customer base shrunk a bit. Some erosion of customer base is expected in the months it takes companies to catch up. Unless there is something unique about its plan, the best AT&T can expect is not to lose any more customers. Going back to impetus of the investment, the successful metric will reflect a post-implementation stabilizing customer base. Then there are investments that are not expected to pay off, such as preventive maintenance, Y2K, and government auditing requirements.

With that in mind, we suggested in Chapter 4 that companies examine case studies of past IT failures—their own as well as those of other companies. It is revealing, as well as humbling, to look back at the causes of failure. User training, lack of communication, buy-in, and participation constitute the most common reason why systems fail. These are core "people" issues that are lost in excessive focus on technology assessment.

Often the true rewards of IT investment are not apparent at the organizational level because something went wrong in the process of converting investment into profits. A shortcoming of past studies has been that they have assumed that an investment in IT will automatically lead to profitability. Chapter 5 discusses a process perspective to measure IT payoff. It proposes that investment should be examined through the assessment of appropriate IT assets, followed by an examination that the IT assets did indeed lead to IT impacts on the intended business function, and finally whether the business function impacted the organization's bottom line. This is also called "conversion effectiveness," or the ability of an organization to convert IT investments into profits.

In Chapter 5, it was recommended to measure IT payoff by examining impacts other than the obvious financial metrics. A balanced scorecard approach considers IT payoff metrics from various perspectives—the customer (how do we look to the customer), internal (what must we excel at), innovation and learning (what can we improve and create value), and financial (how do we look to the shareholder). Considering that an organization is a system made up of several subsystems, each of which affects the others, the BSC helps identify such diverse areas. It also serves as a checklist to ensure that various areas affected by IT change are considered in the payoff examination.

Having examined the metrics involved for IT payoff in various parts of an organization, managers should also understand where the technology lies on the technology S-curve. The S-curve, discussed in Chapter 7, approximates the life cycle of the technology and, therefore, the expected payoff. It estimates the risk as well as the potential for a technology to yield payoff in the future.

While the S-curve measures the maturity stage of information technology, statistical and economic models examine the payoff using quantitative techniques. In Chapter 8, we suggested that cost–benefit analyses and break-even points could determine whether the investment is returning the benefits intended. Net present value (NPV) analysis is applied to assess the value of the payoff by calculating the current value of the investment made over time. Real Options-based approaches attempt to account for the fact that investment over time can be enhanced or terminated based upon the prevailing conditions. The strength of Real Options analysis is its ability to take advantage of new and not previously envisioned opportunities arising out of the initial investment in IT.

With the challenges discussed, the importance of organizational and political issues was highlighted in Chapter 9 through our step-by-step approach to measure IT payoff. The four-phase EIAC model suggests practical steps for instituting a measurement process within organizations. It proposes exploration of opportunities, involvement of people who influence or are affected by the outcomes of IT payoff, data collection and analysis, and finally, communication of IT payoff results to the appropriate people and functions.

The enormous business opportunities afforded by electronic commerce, and the implications for measuring IT payoff, are discussed in Chapter 10. We discuss the challenges and possibilities that lie for measurement of EC investment payoff. Although EC investment is similar to other types of IT investments, the unique metrics and data differentiate it from traditional IT investment.

Finally, in Chapter 11, we present a comprehensive case study of an organization that measured the investment in its IT and set up an ongoing mechanism for capturing appropriate metrics. The case study demonstrates the challenges and the payoff of setting up such a measurement system and eventually incorporating the results in decision making.

Now that you have read the book as well as the recap of the chapters, you may be asking the question, What can I do to start an IT payoff project when I get back to my desk? From this practical perspective we list an action plan with specific steps that combine actionable steps and the EIAC approach described earlier. In addition, we conclude the book with a few other items that will help you implement an ongoing measurement system.

AN ACTION PLAN

An action plan for instituting a payoff mechanism has two sides: (1) what metrics should be captured, and (2) how to implement a measurement system so that the metrics can be captured, analyzed, and used in corporate decision making.

We have discussed developing an approach for assessing the technology payoff through the EIAC model (see Chapter 9). The discussion below builds upon the ingredients of the EIAC model and suggests specific issues, with examples, which should be addressed in developing an action plan. In some ways, our action plan raises more questions for you to consider and find answers to. This is because the IT payoff approach can vary among organizations. In fact, the approach to IT payoff measurement can even vary for the same organization, depending upon the type of investment or the stage of investment.

In Table 12.1, we present several examples of metrics that can be captured depending upon the stage in the process of IT

TABLE 12.1 A Matrix of Sample Operational, Managerial, and Strategic variables for Measuring IT Payoff

	OPERATIONAL IT	MANAGERIAL IT	STRATEGIC IT
Investment	Financial investment in: • FTEs (employees) • Equipment • Consulting	Financial investment and budgeting for: • Applications • Training • Education	Financial investment and budgeting for: • Collaborative technologies • Electronic Data Interchange • ERPs
IT Assets	Number of • Workstations • Automated check-in counters (airlines) • Assembly machines (manufacturing) • Toll processing stations (toll road) • Modems (Insurance adjusters in the field) • Information kiosks (theme parks) • Trainers • Computer-based training • Physical space • Telecommunications infrastructure • Help Desk	Number of • Process redesign projects • Extent of process redesign measured by number of person hours invested and departments involved • Change management initiatives • Managerial reporting infrastructure such as cost accounting applications	Number of • Hubs and routers • Imaging technology • Knowledge-based applications • Teams working on strategic systems • Industry and vendor partnerships • Decision makers • IT payoff measurement process

TABLE 12.1 A Matrix of Sample Operational, Managerial, and Strategic variables for Measuring IT Payoff (Continued)

	OPERATIONAL IT	MANAGERIAL IT	STRATEGIC IT

IT Impacts	Number of
	• Customers serviced
	• Hits on the Web site
	• High-quality pieces produced
	• Problems resolved
	• Satisfied customers
	• Returning customers
	• Customers referred by other customers
	• Orders processed per day
	• Wait times
	• Sales per employee
	• Mean loan approval days
	• Impacts on inventory as measured by:
	  • Rain checks issued
	  • Stock-out complaints
	  • Breakage, spoilage
	  • Special orders placed
		Number of
		• Escalations
		• Missed deadlines
		• Extension of project end dates
		• Reporting errors
		• Technology substitution
		• Mid-project process redesigns
		• Adverse Event Episode detection (healthcare)
		• Product recalls
		• Average length of stay
			• Actual usage by period by user
			• Extent of integration of IT into corporate decision making, such as the number of:
			  • Reports requested
			  • Scenarios analyzed

Organizational Impacts	• Profitability • ROI • ROA	• Employee turnover • Maintenance expense • Downtime • Mortality rate (healthcare)	• Market share • Ranking • Industry awards • Customer service rating • Stock price • Financial rating

payoff measurement. Our intention is not to prescribe a set of metrics; rather, we anticipate that the examples will generate ideas in your mind on what metrics can be captured in your organization.

How to Implement a Measurement System

The success of the IT payoff measurement system depends as much on political and interpersonal persuasiveness as it does on the technical capabilities of the group leading the project. There are legitimate concerns of resource allocation, privacy, and finger pointing after the dust settles. Thus, it is important that the action plan addresses the following issues.

Securing Organizational and Management Commitment

Securing organizational and senior management commitment for IT payoff is usually the first step in initiating the project. The big challenge is how to get senior management's attention toward an IT payoff analysis. As mentioned earlier, if there is organizational "pain," such as a perception that IT investment is not paying off or missed IT implementation deadlines and cost overruns, or competition threatening to take over the customer base, IT payoff analysis is an easy sell. In case business is not feeling the pain, an effort should be made to get management buy-in for the process. In our experience, once the idea is proposed, informally or through a formal proposal, senior management is quick to support it because they have an interest in assessing the value of IT investment and have been asked to do so by the CEO or the board of directors.

The challenge arises when the organization is performing well and business is good. For instance, in the hey-days of the dotcom economy it would have been difficult to convince many companies to conduct a formal analysis of IT spending.

Of course, for some companies such as eBay and Amazon.com, IT *is* the business, and the measurement of IT payoff can appear to be an exercise in futility. To such organizations, the IT payoff analysis can be of greater interest if it yields more information than whether IT investment pays off. The outcomes are likely to get their attention if the payoff is demonstrated in light of organizational imperatives. Past examples of organizational initiatives that have lead to IT payoff have been: (1) teams consisting of five or less people were most successful in IT implementations; (2) IT project teams consisting of a change management facilitator finish projects on time and under budget; and (3) process redesign as a prerequisite to IT investment has shown more pronounced IT payoffs.

In all three situations, finding allies who feel the need and appreciate the results of IT payoff can go a long way in making the project a reality. Furthermore, making the case of organizational benefits, even if the news is not all good, can motivate management to commission the project.

You also have to demonstrate an understanding of the skills required in accomplishing the analysis. This can be demonstrated by preliminary work done by you, or through examples of previously published works by competitors in the industry. A partnership with researchers in a university or trade organization is another way of getting access to specialized analytical skills.

BUILDING DATA PARTNERSHIPS WITH CONSTITUENCIES INSIDE AND OUTSIDE THE ORGANIZATION

Partnership with other constituencies is germane to gathering data for IT payoff measurement. However, accessing the data and getting the cooperation of individuals in various departments is challenging. The challenge becomes especially greater when the data reside outside the organizational structure, such as with customers, suppliers, and business partners. Given that information has a business value, each constituent guards the data to protect the value. Some approaches that have demonstrated usefulness in gathering data are listed below. However, each organization's culture and hierarchy will require customizing one's approach to building partnerships.

"Partnership" is the operative word in gaining access to meaningful data. It is best to involve individuals and departments in the process than to get them to turn over data through a corporate edict. Why? Because it is equally important to know the context of the data, for example, at what point was it collected, what business activity does it represent, what does it not include, or what was the purpose for which it was collected. Answers to these questions maintain the integrity of the analysis and shield the analysts from future embarrassment.

Partnership also means that the provider of the data also has a stake in the outcome of the analysis. This implies that the IT payoff project for which the data are being collected should not pose a threat to the individual, information system, or business function. A common question we get from data keepers is, "Are you measuring the productivity of my department?" Their concern is that if the data did not show an acceptable payoff, the budgets will shrink, or worse. We find that timely and explicit communication can help alleviate such concerns.

Communication plays a critical role in facilitating the project to its successful conclusion. An effective communications plan should:

1. demonstrate organizational commitment to a project
2. specify the intent or need for the project
3. introduce the project team
4. direct various departments to share data with the project members
5. quell fears of negative outcomes
6. list a timetable of when and how the results of the study will be shared with the organization

In projects that require data from outside the organization, it is important to understand the motivation of the other partner(s). If it is to demonstrate the value of a product for sales purposes, then their participation can come with additional baggage, that is, an expectation that results will show a positive payoff when that IT product is implemented. In our experience, it is important to be clear about the objectives of the analysis and not prejudge the outcomes. The results are more defensible if we let the data speak for itself. The analysts should remain open to testing the hypotheses recommended by data providers or outside partners; however, all conclusions should originate from the data.

Often partners in IT payoff analysis are concerned about their data privacy and confidentiality and that of their clients. Furthermore, although in favor of showcasing their work, they are concerned that publication of results may compromise their competitive advantage. We suggest that for any partnerships, analysts or project leaders should be prepared to:

1. sign a nondisclosure agreement (NDA)

2. exclude any references that would identify the partners or their clients

3. disguise the actual numbers and coefficients by multiplying or dividing them with constants

GATHERING DATA

Having secured the buy-in of various constituents, gathering data becomes the next logical step. Gathering data is in many ways a negotiation process with the keepers of that data. There can be tension created between the effort involved and the value of such data. We recommend exploring all sources of data, quantitative as well as qualitative, in the early stages. First, generate a timeline of the events beginning with when the investment need was felt and how long it took to develop a systematic approach to invest, implement, and use the IT assets. Second, identify the users of the IT, people who maintain the IT and understand how to track the data, and those who are responsible for keeping the data. Each of these constituencies will be helpful at various stages of the analysis. Third, to minimize the up-front effort, request samples of each of the data sets available.

The key data sources will depend upon the type of IT (strategic, managerial, or operational), how it is being used (customers, employees), and the objective of the technology (improve productivity, profitability, or customer value). However, we find that certain data will inevitably be needed. We present data items below, followed by examples of sample metrics in Table 12.1.

a. *Accounting and Finance*

Profitability-based metrics: ROI, ROA, net income, profitability per customer, stock price

Productivity-based metrics: Revenue per employee, production per employee, length of stay (hospitals), expenses per employee, accounts receivable days, cash on hand

b. *Manufacturing and Operations*

New product development cycle, time to market, order fulfillment days, extent of process redesign, safety statistics, defective rates, actual usage of the IT

c. *Human Resources*

Employee demographics such as number of years of service, years of experience, functional areas, training, certifications, reporting structure, change management initiatives, seminars, employee education, absenteeism, employee turnover

d. *Marketing or Corporate Development*

Competitive landscape, mergers and acquisitions, strategic plans, market share, number of customers and their demographics, advertising campaigns

Identify the period for each of the data sources. Are data available by week, month, quarter, or year? This is critical for an "apples-to-apples" comparison of investment to payoff data.

Next, investigate the form in which the data are available. Are they in paper reports, completed surveys, computer disks, or online? If online, can data be extracted on demand in a standard format to be read by a standard spreadsheet, database, or statistical package? Can you access the online system to generate the data extract when needed? The answers to these questions will determine how quickly you can get to analyzing the data.

ANALYZING DATA

Once the location and the form of data are determined, the project leaders should review the analytical plan to ensure that the data are sufficient to answer the questions of interest. We find that using the sample data gathered in the earlier stages to conduct a simulated analysis is a practical approach to identifying any future issues.

Our earlier chapters discuss the approach to the payoff analysis by taking into account the type of IT that is being evaluated. It is obvious that the analysis will require profound analytical and business skills. It may be useful to refresh the analytical skills from a business statistics book or other sources of analytical techniques. Furthermore, analytical help can be sought from individuals in finance, quality assurance, or other departments that are well-versed in data analysis approaches.

CAPITALIZING ON THE CASCADING EFFECTS OF IT PAYOFF

The action plan should also look beyond the benefits of measuring IT payoff to second-level benefits that result from such initiatives. Such effects, known as cascading effects, include benefits that flow from one department to another as a result of IT payoff analysis.

The quality assurance department of a large consumer products manufacturing company invested in a computer system to capture and report quality outcomes of various units of the organization. Although the system was developed to fulfill a statutory reporting requirement, the system brought to light significant quality and error rates variation among the various units. In quantifying the payoff from investing in the computer system, it was found that variance existed for similar processes and products across units. This led to the development and dissemination of internal benchmarks for the organization. The cascading effects of the payoff analysis were further capitalized upon when the design and manufacturing departments at various units began interpersonal networking to share best practices and learn from each other. Furthermore, the geographically dispersed customers who were getting inconsistent quality from the various units also began to see consistent quality products. Thus a project that intended to measure the payoff from a reporting system capitalized upon the cascading effects of the technology by exploring other uses of data. Quantifying the benefits of a payoff analysis can sometimes set in motion other uses of the data not envisioned previously.

When developing the action plan, explore additional uses of the information generated by the payoff analysis of an information technology. For example, in conducting the payoff analysis of an operating system upgrade, examine the reduction of downtime and its effect on customer service. Also consider the cost of requests for resend of data placed to other departments due to downtime. Such are the cascading effects of IT payoff analysis. While these effects are not generally attributed to the IT payoff analysis, the exposure of IT benefits beyond the initial intended usage can result from a well-thought-out action plan.

BUILDING AN INFRASTRUCTURE FOR ONGOING IT PAYOFF ANALYSIS

The responsibility of managers does not end with the conclusion of one IT payoff analysis project. Organizations should strive to build the measurement into the systems and the culture of the organization. Although it is clear that measurement of the costs and benefits are easier to capture when data tracking and analysis is built into the system, in most cases the infrastructure for capturing the data is built around existing systems. Pragmatic organizations approach the building of the measurement infrastructure from both ends: modifying existing information systems and mandating that new information systems should provide hooks to gather statistics of usage and other benefits. For example, all training activities should also be captured as and when new users are trained and existing users are given refresher training.

Often the data that constitute costs and benefits for a system are available but scattered across the organization in various stand-alone computer systems or paper reports. Accessing such resources electronically is key to integrating data for payoff analysis and subsequently incorporating them into managerial and strategic decision making.

INTEGRATING IT PAYOFF RESULTS IN MANAGERIAL AND STRATEGIC PLANNING AND DECISION MAKING

Finally, after the infrastructure for data collection and analysis is established, using the results for planning and decision making constitutes the "rubber meets the road" test. While the results of one IT investment payoff analysis may be useful for the evaluation of that particular technology investment, significant benefits await those who take such learning to the planning level. In our experience most organizations fail to do so and are content with the payoff analysis at hand.

How do you integrate the results in planning and decision making? Organizations vary on how they share information with decision makers. However, some steps are critical in accomplishing the integration. First, the results should be communicated to the managers within the organization. You may find an appropriate manner in which the results are made available to managers such that it gets their attention. Often such findings communicated through memos or newsletters go straight to a filing cabinet and never see the light of day! Announcing the findings in an executive council meeting is often an attention-getter while communicating to the contact persons who can supply more information. A follow-up memo or newsletter is usually more effective at this time. Second, cross-trained individuals should be ready and willing to assist managers in understanding the meaning of the findings and demonstrating how they can be tied to their decisions. Creativity on the part of such consultants who can demonstrate the integration with specific examples in functions such as customer service, product design, and operations will be required. Third, the internal consulting activities should be backed up with information systems that deliver payoff outcomes on an ongoing basis.

We visualize the results of IT payoff analysis as one of the indicators on the dashboard of an Executive Information System (EIS), along with manufacturing, sales, customer satisfaction, and profitability indicators. The IT payoff indicators can take the form of return on investment on IT based upon usage of the technology correlated with the quality outcomes metrics described above and in Table 12.1. Usage of this EIS data by decision makers can also be tracked and correlated with improvement in decisions and organizational performance. IT payoff analysis should become part of an organization's toolkit to go beyond the investment justification. Management should demonstrate to employees, business partners, and all stakeholders that it has the know-how to create IT value as well as a mechanism to measure and continuously learn from it.

Index

A

Action plan implementation, 149, 152
    cascading effects, 157–158
    infrastructure for ongoing payoff
        analysis, 158–159
    measurement variables, 150t–151t
Advanced Micro Devices, use of
        balanced scorecards, 56
AIDS-related information tracking, and
        IT investment, 9–10
Amazon.com
    and disparate categories, 125
    and one-to-one marketing, 123
Amos, Jim H., 35
"Appearance" factor, 80
Apple Computer
    and disruptive technologies, 75
    use of balanced scorecards, 56
ASP (application service provider)
        outsourcing companies, 24
Assets–impacts framework (Soh and
        Markus), 44–45, 45f
AT&T, virtual office, 28
autobytel.com, 122

B

Barua, Anitesh and colleagues, 17
    two-stage model, 48–49
BEP (break-even point), 80, 83
Black, Sir James, 66

BPR

BPR (business process reengineering),
    46, 60
    as complementary initiative, 48
Brynjolfsson, Erik, 29, 54, 61
BSC (balanced scorecard approach), 50,
    55, 56f, 59–60, 147–148
    perspectives, 56
        customer, 57
        financial, 59
        innovation and learning, 58–59
        internal business, 57–58
Business value complementarity theory,
    17

C

CAD (computer-aided design), 7
Canon, 75
Center for Research on Information
        Technology and
        Organizations (CRITO),
        18
Christensen, Clayton, 74
Chrysler Corporation, EDI
        implementation study,
        47–48
CIGNA Corporation, and BPR, 46
CIO (chief information officer), 1
Cisco, 127
CNN Interactive, 121
COIN (community of interest) groups,
    124

The *Financial Times* delivers a world of business news.

Use the Risk-Free Trial Voucher below!

To stay ahead in today's business world you need to be well-informed on a daily basis. And not just on the national level. You need a news source that closely monitors the entire world of business, and then delivers it in a concise, quick-read format.

With the *Financial Times* you get the major stories from every region of the world. Reports found nowhere else. You get business, management, politics, economics, technology and more.

Now you can try the *Financial Times* for 4 weeks, absolutely risk free. And better yet, if you wish to continue receiving the *Financial Times* you'll get great savings off the regular subscription rate. Just use the voucher below.

8 reasons why you should read the Financial Times for 4 weeks RISK-FREE!

To help you stay current with significant
developments in the world economy ...
and to assist you to make informed business
decisions — the Financial Times brings you:

❶ Fast, meaningful overviews of international affairs ... plus daily
briefings on major world news.

❷ Perceptive coverage of economic, business, financial and political
developments with special focus on emerging markets.

❸ More international business news than any other publication.

❹ Sophisticated financial analysis and commentary on world market
activity plus stock quotes from over 30 countries.

❺ Reports on international companies and a section on global investing.

❻ Specialized pages on management, marketing, advertising and
technological innovations from all parts of the world.

❼ Highly valued single-topic special reports (over 200 annually)
on countries, industries, investment opportunities, technology and more.

❽ The Saturday Weekend FT section — a globetrotter's guide to
leisure-time activities around the world: the arts, fine dining, travel,
sports and more.

For Special Offer See Over

FT FINANCIAL TIMES
World business newspaper